Mississippi Bishop
William Henry Elder
and the Civil War

MISSISSIPPI BISHOP
WILLIAM HENRY ELDER
and the Civil War

RYAN STARRETT | *Foreword by Cleta Ellington*

THE
History
PRESS

Published by The History Press
Charleston, SC
www.historypress.net

First published 2019

Manufactured in the United States

ISBN 9781467143806

Library of Congress Control Number: 2019945085

This book is dedicated to my five womb fellows:

Mary-Catherine, an exemplary mother who bravely campaigns for those suffering from mental illnesses.
Reid, who plays with angels and saints and constantly intercedes for the rest of us.
Caitlin, who tirelessly advocates on behalf of children stuck in the foster system.
Callaghan, who crisscrosses the country raising two young, energetic children of her own, armed only with coffee.
Reilly, who travels the world in search of Truth.

Table of Contents

Foreword, by Cleta Ellington   9
Preface   11
Acknowledgements   13
Introduction   15

1. The Appointment   17
2. The Soldier-Sheep   26
3. The Ghosts of Battle   28
4. October 28 to November 16, 1862   35
5. Flashback: Childhood and Parents   41
6. November 19, 1862, to February 23, 1863   45
7. The *Queen of the West*   54
8. February 25 to July 6, 1863   58
9. Meanwhile…in Vicksburg   66
10. July 7 to July 20, 1863   76
11. St. Peter's Becomes a Relic of "Chimneyville"   82
12. July 20 to July 24, 1863   86
13. The Battle   90
14. July 24 to September 16, 1863   101
15. The Hospitals   127
16. September 17 to October 25, 1863   136
17. December 22, 1863, to June 25, 1864   143
18. June 26 to August 13, 1864   156

19. August 14 to December 27, 1864   170
20. The Occupation   176
21. December 27, 1864, to March 27, 1865   180

Conclusion   187
Notes   189
Works Cited   205
About the Author   208

FOREWORD

O h, those are the smart Starretts!"
That is what U.S. District Judge Keith Starrett said when I told him how much I had enjoyed teaching four of the children of his cousin Richard and Mary Reid Starrett at St. Joseph Catholic School in Madison. Truthfully, the Starretts I taught—Ryan and his sisters Mary Catherine, Caitlin and Callaghan—would be the smart ones in anyone's family. They were eager learners who loved words, books, art, ideas and asking questions that challenged their teachers.

Those smart Starretts made a better teacher out of me, none more so than Ryan, who has had the pure heart of a genuine scholar for as long as I have known him. In seventh grade, in fact, Ryan was so fascinated by the American Revolution that I sent him a postcard of a militia man I bought on a trip to Concord—the only student I have ever sent a summer postcard to in over thirty years of teaching.

I can imagine Ryan's excitement when he opened the pages of Bishop William Henry Elder's Civil War Diary, because that small red volume is one of the treasures of the Diocesan Archive in the basement of the Catholic Chancery on Amite Street in Jackson. I remember how excited I was to read it thirty-five years ago, when I was researching parish histories for the *Mississippi Today* (now the *Mississippi Catholic*), the weekly newspaper of the Jackson Diocese.

Elder's entries are brief, but Ryan's scholarship fills in the blanks, giving historical context to events the bishop recorded. Ryan's choices of primary source material give voice to people Elder mentions in his diary as he goes about his often grueling days.

Like all diarists, Elder is a faithful recorder of the weather, especially bad weather. One of the things I like best about this book is the way Ryan uses the weather to set the stage for miserable events often made more miserable by miserable Mississippi weather (which ring very familiar, even today).

As we read Ryan's book, we meet people thrust from their ordinary lives into war: a handful of intrepid European-born missionaries who find themselves comforting wounded and dying soldiers in addition to serving Catholics scattered across 48,000 square miles of wilderness; Sisters of Mercy transformed from convent-school teachers into battlefield nurses; Vicksburg families of every social and economic strata hunkering down in self-dug caves in the bluffs to escape bombardment; Confederate and Federal officers, wartime civil authorities, whom Elder must placate on behalf of his flock; landed gentry newly bereft of loved ones and livelihood; and the most tragic, hundreds of newly freed slaves dying of starvation, filth and disease in hastily organized Federal "corrals" in Vicksburg and Natchez.

So, this is not a typical Civil War history. There is very little attention paid to military actions, and none at all paid to powerful generals. A hero abides, though. Through Ryan Starrett's mastery of his craft, we come to know Bishop William Henry Elder as a real person: loyal, traditional, savvy, conflicted, sometimes lonely, always compassionate—a man who never wasted the opportunity to hear the confession of a soldier about to go into battle, a shepherd of souls.

Writing histories is not Ryan Starrett's day job. He teaches eleventh-grade religion at St. Joseph in Madison. His curriculum is the Sacraments and Dante. (Typical of Ryan, that juxtaposition!) My hope for him is that he finds students whom he never wants to disappoint, because that was the standard I held myself to on his behalf. My great hope is that one of his students will make him as grateful as "Warrior Bishop" has made me.

—Cleta Ellington, author and retired teacher

PREFACE

The language of the following book is often times anachronistic and sometimes blatantly racist, but it is true to the times in which Bishop William Henry Elder lived. Reading the diary entries of 1860s Southerners (and Northerners, too) frequently makes one cringe. "Negroes," "coloreds," "chattel," "darkies" and "contraband"—as offensive as they might be—were terms regularly used in the historical record. However, the answer is not to whitewash the offending phrases but to accurately record the sentiments of the time.

Additionally, the attitude of most white persons toward black persons at the time fell into one of three categories, sometimes overlapping: paternalistic, ignorant or racist. Their viewpoints are reflected in their writings. Again, it is important to record these views, because they allow us into the mind of the largest segment of the population in the United States of the mid-nineteenth century. Understanding a person's rationale—with its fears, dreams and prejudices—opens the door to discourse and education. Demonizing them shuts the door to dialogue and reconciliation.

Finally, the cruelty of many who fought for the Union and the insensitivity of the federal government to the plight of the freedmen does not suggest that the Southern approach to race relations was better, as it most certainly was not.

War is evil, and it brings out the worst in men. But it is inevitable as long as men inhabit the earth, and when it erupts, a good bishop will summon his clergy and send his warrior clerics into battle—not to slay his fellow man but to bless, instruct, console and forgive.

Acknowledgements

I would like to thank all those historians, researchers, archivists, teachers, artists and photographers who came before me and paved the way for a project like this. I thank them for allowing me to stand on their shoulders and see the history of my home state through their own work.

I would like to extend a special thanks to those directly involved in this project—Joe Gartrell, the acquisitions editor at The History Press; the Catholic Diocese of Jackson Archives, particularly Mary Woodward; Newspapers.com for creating such an amazing research tool; Richard Starrett for the editing and for not telling me the lie that everything I write is perfect just the way it is; Sara Evans for being equally critical in the editing process and correcting a number of mistakes; Cleta Ellington for her contributions, but even more importantly, for her decades as a teacher at St. Joseph High School; Josh Foreman, with whom I've written two previous books with The History Press and who greatly aided with the photographs found in this book; St. Joseph School for giving me a dream job and a schedule that enables me to both teach and write; and my students, who make each day so enjoyable.

INTRODUCTION

THE DIARY

On a bitterly cold morning, near the end of October 1862, Bishop William Henry Elder of the Catholic Diocese of Natchez, Mississippi, began his Civil War diary. The war had been going on for more than a year, and it had become clear that it would last much longer than many of his state's ardent secessionists had promised when they first formed their rebel government.

While the war in Virginia had been going relatively well for the Confederacy and the Mississippians fighting there, the war on the western front had not been going so well. By October 1862, Mississippi had already been invaded from the north. Vicksburg had been bombarded. New Orleans was in Federal hands. A blockade was suffocating the coast, and two bloody battles at Shiloh and Corinth had sent shock waves through the state.

The spring and summer of 1862 changed the course of the war, and henceforward, Mississippi would become inseparably linked to the Union's ascendency and the Confederacy's doom. As the shepherd of a flock that encompassed the entire state, Bishop Elder—and his clerics—would play a pivotal role as participants in and observers of the crisis that engulfed their state.

1

THE APPOINTMENT

On May 3, 1857, in his home state of Maryland, William Henry Elder received his marching orders. On the same day he was appointed to take charge of the fledgling diocese of Natchez, Mississippi, he was ordained its bishop. The next twenty-two years of his life would be full of romance and joy, progress and war, sickness and destruction, ruin and reconstruction. Natchez was both the vocation and the cross for William Henry Elder.

———

Natchez, the city that would become Elder's home for more than twenty-two years, already had an established reputation when he arrived. It was known both for its opulence and its violence. It was home to the dregs of the Mississippi River traffic and to some of the richest men in the nation. It harbored and nurtured scoundrels and serial killers at the same time it was home to a who's who of United States culture. James Burr, John Murrell, James Audubon, Andrew Jackson and scores of other villains and icons had wandered its streets.

Despite the wealth and history of Natchez, the Mississippi legislature voted to move the state capital to a more centralized location, and the administrative center of the state moved ninety miles east, to Jackson, in 1822. Yet Natchez remained the episcopal see, the headquarters, of the Catholic presence in Mississippi.

Andrew Jackson. *Library of Congress.*

Left: John James Audubon in the 1820s. *Library of Congress.*

Right: John Murrell, based on a print. *Cincinnati Digital Library.*

A large diocese (in terms of land), a spread-out population and a see that was no longer the capital of the state meant that Elder would be on the road—something that didn't bother the young and energetic bishop.

———

The thirty-seven-year-old bishop arrived at his see on May 30, 1857, with "soft breezes blowing across the Mississippi River." He was the only native-born cleric in his entire diocese. Seven of his priests came from France,

A young William Henry Elder. *Archives of the Diocese of Jackson.*

three from Ireland, one from Belgium and one from Saxony (in present-day Germany). In fact, Elder inherited about as many priests as siblings he had left behind in Maryland. He had grown up in a household with six brothers, three sisters and two or three orphans living under the same roof. Now, he had a dozen clerics responsible for the salvation of an entire state.[1]

One of his first acts as bishop was to appoint Father Mathurin Grignon as his vicar general, or representative. This would allow Elder to immediately travel the entirety of his extensive diocese. The odyssey would both familiarize him with his new home and introduce himself to his flock, both religious and lay.[2]

Elder completed his marathon inspection of the diocese and learned several significant facts. The Catholics of Mississippi formed a microcosm of the state. They stood upon all rungs of the economic and social ladder, from slave to subsistence farmer to professor to state legislator. Just about the time Elder assumed his see, large numbers of Irish people migrated to the state and took jobs as railroad and levee workers. Of the ten thousand Catholics in the diocese—7 percent of the population of Mississippi—one thousand were slaves. In all, Elder had eleven parishes with eleven churches

Natchez in the 1850s—the Bluff and Under-the-Hill are both clearly visible. *The Beinecke Library at Yale University.*

Elms Court, Natchez, Mississippi—residence of the Honorable A.P. Merrill, 1850s. *Metropolitan Museum of Art.*

A ship at rest beneath one of the Natchez Bluffs in 1864. *Library of Congress.*

and twenty-eight mission stations, and only a dozen priests to tend them. It was destined to be a busy two decades for the energetic bishop.

———

The biggest challenge to Elder's episcopacy was the threat of a looming civil war. It was not the first time the horrors of a fraternal war threatened the unity of his homeland. A significant number of New Englanders had threatened secession in the midst of the War of 1812. Large numbers of Westerners made similar threats to join the ambiguous Burr-Wilkinson alliance that, if successful, might have sundered the West from the infant nation. John C. Calhoun imperiled the Union with constant rhetoric involving state's rights and nullification. Now, a new brand of fire-eaters promised secession if the institution of slavery was not protected and extended.

From his installation in 1857 to the presidential election in 1860, Elder remained on the sidelines, as did nearly every American bishop. The ecclesiastical provinces of Baltimore and Cincinnati summarized the Catholic position regarding the role of the clergy in the secession debate. The former stated: "Our clergy have wisely abstained from all interference with the judgement of the faithful, which should be free on all questions of polity and social order, within the limits of the doctrines of Christ."[3] The latter proclaimed: "While the Church's ministers rightfully feel a deep and abiding interest in all that concerns the welfare of the country, they do not think it their province to enter into the political arena."[4] Bishop Elder adopted the same stance. Neither he nor his priests promoted nor condemned secession. That was a matter for the laity (nonclergy) to decide.

Although he kept his thoughts to himself, Elder prayed for peace. If secession could occur peacefully, so be it. If not, then war was always a great evil—necessary sometimes, as his church's just war theory set forth,[5] but always ugly and vile and to be avoided at nearly all costs. War interrupted the day-to-day business of saving souls. It introduced chaos into the public order, and it imposed upon churches, schools and charitable institutions.[6] Not to mention, it frequently demonized the enemy and dehumanized the soldiers of one's own side.

Finally, Elder's desire for peace would have been strengthened by the fact that both Natchez and Vicksburg—the two Mississippi cities with the largest concentrations of Catholics—were full of hopeful Unionists. They were wealthy cities with politically powerful merchants who relied upon the cotton trade and an open Mississippi River. War, or even the threat of war, would endanger their pocketbooks. Thus, Elder, though in an ardent secessionist diocese, spent the majority of his days leading up to 1860 surrounded by Southern Union men.[7]

In the weeks leading up to the secession convention, Elder sent a circular letter to his priests instructing them to offer prayers and Masses that the legislators would receive heavenly wisdom before the upcoming convention. He also implemented a diocesan-wide fast for each Friday of Advent.[8] Unlike many of his Protestant counterparts, Elder didn't tell his priests to urge their flocks to vote one way or another. He simply prayed that the legislators would vote the right way. What that "right" way was, Elder never mentioned publicly—if he even knew himself.[9]

Ultimately, Elder's handling of the secession question can be summed up in a letter he wrote to his cobishop and friend Francis Kenrick, of Baltimore, Maryland:

> *My course, & I believe the course of my clergy, has been not to recommend secession—but to explain to those who might enquire, that—if they were satisfied, dispassionately—that secession was the only practical remedy, the only means of safety—their religion did not forbid them to advocate it—on the contrary they were bound to do, what they believed the safety of the community required.*[10]

Some of Elder's flock sided with the Unionists, some with the secessionists. The latter garnered the necessary votes, and Mississippi officially seceded from the United States on January 9, 1861. Once it was clear that a new state government—and, on March 29, 1861, a functioning Confederate government—would be established, Elder urged his flock to support the new authority. He wrote a letter to the bishop of Chicago, James Duggan, explaining his decision to stand by the new Confederate States of America:

> *I hold it is the duty of all Catholics in the seceeding* [sic] *states to adhere to the actual government without reference to the right or the wisdom of making the separation—or to the grounds for it:—our State governments & our new Confederation are de facto our only existing government here, & it seems to me that as good Citizens we are bound not only—to acquiesce to it—but to support it, & contribute means & arms.*[11]

Shortly after, Elder wrote to Bishop Kenrick:

> *Since secession has been accomplished—I have advised even those who thought it unwise—still to support our State Govt. & the new Confederacy—as being the only Govts. which exist here de facto. I have encouraged all to give a hearty support—to enrol [sic] as soldiers—to go forward with their taxes—to co-operate in any way they had occasion for.*[12]

For better or worse, the Confederate States provided the functioning government of Mississippi. Right or wrong, it was this government that could provide security and stability. It was the authority that controlled the police forces, collected taxes and oversaw the day-to-day functions of civic life. Elder, who, like most Catholic leaders, feared anarchy, cast his lot with the state of Mississippi and the Confederate government.

As the war progressed, Bishop Elder hardened in his defense of his adopted state. He wrote to Bishop Duggan in Chicago:

> *Above all I could not accept the term disloyalty as applicable to the course of our Southern People. Without discussing whether the grounds for our separation…were before God sufficient or not—they certainly were such as honest men might easily accept as sufficient. And from what I have seen & heard, I am satisfied that the great body of the people have acted conscientiously according to their sense of duty.—It is a great mistake in the north to imagine our people are rushing on in an excitement of passion.*[13]

Within two years, Elder would see the futility of secession. He would also see the heartlessness of many Northern commanders, causing him to love his people and his state ever more deeply. However, the bishop's devotion to his flock and homeland never caused him to embrace the die-hard, fight-to-the-death mentality that blinded so many of the South's leaders. Instead, Elder remained a voice of moderation and mutual respect throughout the war. He interacted with and ministered to Federal troops just as he did to Confederates. Likewise, he instructed his priests to account for the souls of both Federal and Confederate troops.

Elder coat of arms. *Archives of the Diocese of Jackson.*

24

Such personal moderation rubbed off on Elder's priests. All of his diocesan priests mirrored the sentiments of their bishop, in word and action. Even those priests who would serve as military chaplains drew a strict line between "the Cause" and their own cause for accompanying the troops—to offer consolation in times of distress and death and to lead souls—Confederate and Yankee—to heaven.[14]

2

THE SOLDIER-SHEEP

On October 28, 1862, two days after Bishop William Henry Elder began his journal, he received ominous news from Frederick, Maryland, the state where he was born. A Miss Marcilly wrote that twenty-four-year-old Frank Arrighi was at her house recovering from the Battle of South Mountain.[15]

The story of Frank Arrighi was typical of many of Elder's laymen with one notable exception: Frank Arrighi would survive the war mostly intact.

FRANK ARRIGHI

It was good to be a soldier. The romance, the camaraderie, the glory. Frank Arrighi, of Natchez, Mississippi, was only too happy to be one of the envied few, the pride of his hometown.

It was a glorious Mississippi River town morning. "A more beautiful day…we do not recollect to have witnessed. The sky was clear, unfrocked with a single cloud, the sun shown [*sic*] out with brilliancy, though without the summer's fervor, the streets and clouds were hard and dry, and all Nature seemed to wear a smile." It was 1859, the anniversary of the forming of the Adams Light Guard, and in the morning, the troop marched through all the principal streets of Natchez to a "romantic looking pine grove" about a mile south of old Fort Rosalie. There, around one o'clock in the afternoon, the soldiers were served a feast consisting of "a bountiful supply of sumptuous soldiers' fare [that] made its appearance in sundry and divers messes to which one and all, hosts and guests, did ample justice." Cheers erupted when pound cakes, along with kegs of beer and champagne, were wheeled into the temporary encampment.[16]

After enjoying the hearty meal and drinks, the soldiers showed off their marksmanship during a target-shooting competition. The citizens of Natchez, those not fortunate enough to be soldiers, watched and cheered for their favorites. The city had established five prizes for the top marksmen. Frank Arrighi took home the third-place prize: a "richly chased silver cup." The Adams Light Guard wound up a morning and afternoon of great frivolity with one final march through their beloved hometown just before sunset.[17]

Yes, it was grand to be a soldier.

Three years later, Sergeant Thomas S. Sheridan wrote a letter to his wife in Natchez that she shared with the local paper. It read: "We (the 16th Miss. Regiment) took into the action, on the morning of the battle, 227 men, and came out with only 81—having 146 killed and wounded."[18]

One of the wounded was Lieutenant Frank Arrighi, the sharpshooter and pride of Natchez, who had been shot in the head. The company's captain, Edward C. Councill, informed the citizens of Natchez, including Arrighi's family, friends and bishop, that their Frank had suffered a severe head wound.[19]

One month later, Captain Councill wrote home, informing Natchez that Arrighi was in an enemy camp but walking around and doing better.[20]

Evidently, the young lieutenant was either paroled or part of a prisoner exchange, for he traveled home to Natchez for a five-month respite. After visiting his bishop, friends and family, Arrighi returned to his company in Virginia. The twenty-four-year-old soldier had already done his part in the war effort. He had been in a number of engagements in which he had served with distinction and been severely wounded and medically furloughed, and he was now returning for more.[21]

Through letters and visits, Bishop Elder would stay abreast of Frank Arrighi's trials throughout the war. Now, on this cold day in October 1862, all he knew was that his parishioner lay a thousand miles away recovering from a grievous wound.

THE GHOSTS OF BATTLE

Bishop Elder would go on to receive countless letters and obituaries regarding his soldier flock. He was, like most in the United States, unprepared for the carnage that would engulf the country for four long years. He received his first forecast of the hell that is war when reports began to flood in about a great battle fought next to a small Tennessee church just across the border from his diocese. Elder had sent a handful of priests north in anticipation of the fight. Then, during the first week of May 1862, he traveled north to offer what succor he could.

SHILOH

The bishop visited the area one month after the battle. Although he was not a participant nor an eyewitness himself, Elder, along with Fathers Elia, Pont and Leray, did see the aftermath of the staggering slaughter. Hundreds of his diocesan flock and thousands of his coreligionists were direct partakers in one of the Western Hemisphere's bloodiest days.

Henry Morton Stanley, of "Dr. Livingstone, I presume?" fame, fought for the Confederacy on that fateful day and left behind a vivid and powerful description of what the common soldier went through. Stanley had taken shelter behind a fallen tree when his units' charge faltered under devastating defensive fire from the Union troops. He wrote:

I marveled, as I heard the unremitting patter, snip, thud, and hum of bullets, how anyone could live under this raining death. I could hear the bullets beating a merciless tattoo on the outer surface of the log, pinging viciously as they flew off at a tangent to it, and thudding into something or other at the rate of a hundred a second. One here, one there found its way under the log and buried itself in a comrade's body.

One man raised his chest as if to yawn and jostled me. I turned to him and saw that a bullet had gored his whole face and penetrated into his chest. Another ball struck a man a deadly rap upon the head, and he turned on his back and showed his ghastly white face to the sky. [Another] raised his head a little too high, when a bullet skimmed over the top of the log and hit him fairly in the center of his forehead and he fell on his face.[22]

The intensity of the fight and subsequent terror experienced by Stanley was representative of the experiences of the ordinary soldier that day, as

The Battle of Shiloh, by A.E. Mathews, showing a charge and the taking of a New Orleans battery by the Fourteenth Regiment Wisconsin Volunteers on Monday, April 7, 1862. *Library of Congress.*

Mississippi private Augustus Hervey Mecklin confirmed. Mecklin recalled marching toward the sound of battle, passing dead, dying and wounded Confederates, then Yankees, then a mixture of the two, "some torn to mincemeat by canon [*sic*] balls. Some still writhing in the agonies of death." And yet, they continued to march toward the sound of the dueling cannon. During a brief respite, the regiment halted, and one of Mecklin's comrades leaned against a tree. A Federal cannonball struck the tree "nearly a foot through & splitting it asunder tore a poor fellow who was behind it into nearly a thousand pieces. We moved on."[23]

In spite of the terrible carnage around him, Mecklin was struck with the utter beauty of nature. Then he remembered—it was Sunday morning.

> *It was very warm. The sky was clear and but for the horrible monster death who now piled high carnival, this might have been such a Sabbath morn as would have called pleasant recollections of Sabbath bells and religious enjoyment.... The sight was beautiful, viewed aside from the scenes of blood*

The Battle of Shiloh, by J.H. Bufford, is a lithograph showing the Battle of Shiloh (or Pittsburg Landing), which took place on April 6 and 7, 1862. *Library of Congress.*

that now surrounded it. The country was level. The trees were budding into the first leaf of spring.[24]

The body count continued to rise, and the wounded continued to scream in agony, on this beautiful Sunday morning.

Tens of thousands of soldiers, mostly untested, were a part of the sacrifice that was Shiloh. The two day battle led to 23,741 combined casualties—more than those of the American Revolution, War of 1812 and Mexican-American War combined. The Confederates lost 1,723 killed, 8,012 wounded and 959 missing or captured. It was a horrific revelation that the war of secession was doomed to continue into the foreseeable future, and both sides seemed willing to pay the butcher's bill.[25]

As ugly as the fighting had been on April 6 and 7, 1862, the aftermath was equally disturbing. Although it is only a possibility that Bishop Elder and Fathers Pont and Leray had visited the battlefield itself once the fighting ceased, it is a certainty that they would have seen the thousands of casualties. They were firsthand witnesses to the horrors of a new style of warfare in which advances in weaponry and the ability to kill reached unprecedented levels.

Although Elder was not present for the battle, other chaplains certainly were. In fact, one of them, M. Leander Weller, an Episcopalian chaplain attached to the Ninth Mississippi Regiment, was killed while giving aid to a wounded comrade.[26] Later in the war, witnesses verified the presence of Father Leray at the Battle of Raymond. The chaplains who chose to accompany their units into battle, whether to give moral support or to spend the last moments with the dying, ran the same risks as the combatants. By the end of the war, forty-one Confederate chaplains had been killed while on duty, including ten from Mississippi.[27] One priest, Father P. Emmeran Bliemel, of the Tenth Tennessee Regiment, was killed while performing his priestly duties during the Battle of Jonesboro in 1864. While giving last rites to a mortally wounded colonel, Father Bliemel was decapitated by a Federal cannonball.[28] Battlefield bullets and shells were no respecter of clerical rank.

Henry Morton Stanley was fortunate to survive the battle with only a slight stomach wound from a spent bullet that dented his belt buckle. Thus, he was able to record his observations of the post-battle grounds. He saw close to two dozen bodies "lying in various postures, each by its own pool of viscous blood, which emitted a peculiar scent, which was new to me.… Beyond these, a still larger group lay, body overlying body." He continued to traverse a field with "those wide-open dead eyes." He reflected that this "was the first Field of Glory I had seen…and the first time that Glory sickened me with its repulsive aspect, and made me suspect it was all a glittering lie."[29]

Musician fourth class John Cockerill of the Federal forces also partook of his first battle that day and was just as horrified as his Confederate counterpart when traversing the bloodied field. His reminiscences are worth reading at length:

> *In places the bodies of the slain lay upon the ground so thick that I could step from one to the other…I remember a poor Confederate lying upon his back, while by his side was a heap of ginger cakes and bologna sausage. [He] had evidently filled his pockets the day before with edibles from a sutler's tent and had been killed before he had an opportunity to enjoy [them].*
>
> *[I] passed the corpse of a beautiful boy in gray, who lay with his blond curls scattered about his face, and his hands folded peacefully about his chest. He was clad in a bright, neat uniform, well garnished with gold, which seemed to tell the story of a loving mother and sisters who had sent their household pet to the field of war. He was about my age…*
>
> *The blue and the gray were mingled together, side by side. Beneath a great oak tree I counted the corpses of fifteen men, lying as though during the night, suffering from wounds, they had crawled together for mutual assistance, and there all had died.*[30]

Observations like Stanley's and Cockerill's litter the diaries of the soldiers who fought at Shiloh—at least, those who survived the carnage.

Augustus Hervey Mecklin was one such survivor. His fascination with the beauty of the natural world around him during the first day's battle turned to horror that night.

> *About midnight we were awakened, with orders to fall in. The rain began to fall in torrents. The darkness was so intense that I could scarcely see my file leader. Passing on the more gloomy sights and sounds I could scarcely imagine. I have said it was dark, but frequent vivid peals of flashings of lightening [sic] rent the heavens & revealed objects clearly all around.*[31]

Each time the "lightening" flashed, Mecklin beheld a sickening sight—sometimes a mutilated soldier, sometimes a corpse spread across his path, sometimes a man lying in swamp water. During one flash, he saw the rain pelting the forehead of a dead soldier and reflected: "Perhaps a brow often kissed by fond & loving sister, mother or wife, who now await for the dear objects of their love, no longer to feel their kind manifestations of love." Later, "as the light of heaven flashed across this scene of blood I saw a large piece of ground literally covered with dead heaped & piled upon each other. I shut my eyes upon the sickening sight [b]ut a loud moan came to my ears crying 'water, water…O for a little water.'" Mecklin's unit marched on but a little ways when they were ordered to halt for the night and take what rest they could amongst the dead and dying.[32]

Even in death, the deceased did not find peace. As the battle wound down, huge herds of man-eating hogs appeared on the battlefield and began to devour dead and wounded alike. One diarist grew nauseated when he heard the "unmistakable quarreling over their carnival feast." Another recoiled in horror at the sight of the descending hordes of feral hogs. Later, Mrs. Duncan, who owned land near the Shiloh battlefield, claimed, "The Yankees did not bury the Confederate dead. They threw them into the gullies and ravines and covered them with leaves and left them for the hogs to root and eat up. I know this to be the truth. I could not understand anyone to be so heartless to leave a human being unburied even if they were a rebel—they were dead."[33]

The Battle of Shiloh, with the gunboats *Tylor* [i.e. *Tyler*] and *Lexington* supporting the Federal troops. *Library of Congress.*

For those who walked the field of battle days or even weeks later, the psyche-altering sights of warfare were still visible. Many of the dead were not buried deep enough, and their arms, legs and heads were, in many cases, protruding above the grave. A month later, Federal troops marching on Corinth via the Shiloh battlefield reported the sickening stench and the throngs of bluebottle flies.[34]

Bishop Elder and his fellow clerics had received a vivid and gruesome foreshadowing of what the next three years would entail. The aftermath of Shiloh would haunt Elder for the duration of the war and make him even more sensitive to the needs of his soldier-sheep.

4

OCTOBER 28 TO
NOVEMBER 16, 1862

Six months later, the horrors of Shiloh still distressed Elder. News from the hospitals was a constant reminder. The same day he received the unfortunate news regarding Frank Arrighi, Bishop Elder learned from Father Francis Xavier Leray that the hospital at Holly Springs would soon be closing. The sick had been treated, limbs amputated and the wounded sent home. Elder suggested that the nuns working at the hospital make their way to Sulphur Springs, where their services might be put to better use.

All of Elder's worries were diverted on November 1 as he prepared for one of his church's largest feast days of the year—All Saints' Day. On this day, as the world he knew was more uncertain than it had been since his birth, the bishop took refuge in the eighteen and a half centuries of his church's history. He preached about the divinity of his church; the communion of saints; the one continuous line from the time of the Apostles to his own; the sacrifices of the martyrs; the succession of popes, from Peter to Pius IX; the permanence of the Sacraments over the last 1,800 years: "She is still the same Church—wishing to make Saints now—'tis her whole business—and we are the material—just like the other Saints—to be perfected by the same means if we will use them."[35] Perhaps Elder was subconsciously reminding himself of the glories of his universal church even while his particular diocese was experiencing a time of turbulence, perhaps he was merely preaching on a set of liturgical readings that

Pope Pius IX Imparting the Blessing Urbi et Orbi by François-Léon Benouville. *Metropolitan Museum of Art.*

happened to fall on that day or perhaps he was convincing himself of the permanence of an institution (in which he was a leader) in the midst of upheaval. That afternoon, Bishop Elder canceled evening prayers in order to hear more confessions.[36]

On All Souls' Day—November 2, which happened to fall on a Sunday in 1862—Elder again celebrated an important Mass.[37] The bishop prayed for all the souls who had already departed the battlefield of earth. In the next three years—from 1863 to 1865—this particular Mass would become far, far more meaningful to Bishop Elder, his clergy and the people of Mississippi.

Between the All Saints' and All Souls' Masses, Elder estimated that he distributed between 240 and 260 Hosts.[38] These sacramental Hosts can only be consumed by the forgiven. Evidently, his decision to extend the confessional hours the night before paid off, and evidently, the Catholics of his parish felt—more than ever—a sense of their own mortality.

After the All Souls' midmorning Mass, the bishop went to the cemetery at 3:30 p.m. While there, he sang the De Profundis and Magnificat for the departed souls. He then sang the Litany of the Saints before giving his sermon in the graveyard.

Five days later, on the following Friday, life went on as usual. Elder visited his parish school. While the storm clouds settled in the northern portions of his diocese, Bishop Elder was giving exams at Miss Kate's school. He tested the students on their catechism, grammar, spelling, history, reading, geography and Latin. For three and a half hours, the students impressed their bishop—for the most part. That evening, Elder wrote: "Very manifest improvement in every class except one of Geography which failed entirely.—The Grammar & History showed most improvement."[39] The bishop surely went to bed pleased with the day. The war had already taken too many young Catholics in his sparsely populated diocese. There was no telling how many more would be killed before peace was restored. Elder knew this challenge was going to be difficult to overcome. He knew another war would begin when the current one ended and his state was reconstructed under either the Stars and Stripes or the Stars and Bars. Either way, the Catholic Church in Mississippi would need a new generation of educated leaders to replace all those slain fathers lying buried on distant battlefields.

With the dead soldiers still on his mind, Bishop Elder offered a requiem Mass on their behalf the day after the exams.[40]

FATHER PHILIP HUBER

The following Monday, Father Huber visited Elder to inform him that he had been accepted as chaplain to the Tenth Tennessee Regiment. Elder was stunned. Father Huber was a sickly man. Furthermore, he had already seen his fair share of suffering and death, having been present at Holly Springs and Oxford during the aftermath of Shiloh. Elder reasoned that Father Huber was attempting to excuse himself from the financial worries that besieged his parish, Port Gibson—the church was unfinished, and the congregation had shrunk to six persons on account of the war.

Bishop Elder misread the character of his priest. He promised him an easier post. He wrote: "If you find your health cannot stand that method of life, you must leave it.…I think I can find a place for you without your returning to Port Gibson."[41] Father Huber refused. Instead, he marched to battle with the Tenth Tennessee Regiment.

Just before departing with his regiment, Father Huber returned to Port Gibson, paid off what debt he could afford and headed north to pay his

The Windsor Mansion ruins in Port Gibson, Mississippi, by Carol M. Highsmith. *Library of Congress.*

respects and bid farewell to his bishop. Prudently, he also picked up some warm clothing in Natchez. He would need it in the upcoming months.

On November 12, Father Huber rejoined the Tenth Tennessee. He was still a noncommissioned chaplain, per the wishes of his bishop. Elder preferred his chaplains not accept official positions in the CSA army. He believed the democratic process for selecting a chaplain led to the election of a mostly Protestant chaplaincy. However, many Catholics were serving and therefore did not have access to a Catholic minister. If the Catholic priests retained their "roving" status, they would be able to meet the needs of Catholics in units throughout the army. Elder and Bishop John Quinlan of Mobile sent a joint request to the CSA War Department asking that Catholic chaplains be formally commissioned but granted freedom of movement throughout an entire army rather than being restricted to a particular regiment. The War Department never responded, and throughout the war, Elder insisted that his clerics reject official commissions in order to safeguard their availability to the maximum number of troops. (The poet laureate of the Confederacy, Father Abram Joseph Ryan, who spent time in Elder's diocese in Biloxi, would remain one of these unattached priests throughout the war—like "those other priests from Natchez to Mobile who remain shadowy figures on the fringes of Civil War history."[42])

Father Huber's first three months of service vacillated between mundane, uncomfortable camp life and the freedom of mobility. He bivouacked with his regiment for about a month, and when the rain and cold weather made martial conflict unlikely, he headed south to rejoin his bishop in Natchez.[43]

Two weeks later, he was riding north toward the fighting at Chickasaw Bayou near Vicksburg. When the dust settled, Father Huber elected to remain with the Tenth Tennessee, which he did until he contracted fever and dysentery. By then, it had become clear to Elder that Father Huber was, in fact, not physically fit for the life of a military chaplain, and the bishop reassigned his zealous priest to pastor the churches in Sulphur Springs and Canton.[44]

———

Memories of Shiloh came to haunt the bishop again on the next day. Lieutenant Hart of the Natchez Southrons—a distinctively Catholic company—visited the bishop and informed Elder of events in Kentucky. The Confederate army had been forced to retreat, its high expectations dashed.

The Battle of Corinth, which took place on October 3 and 4, 1862. *Library of Congress.*

Lieutenant Hart blamed the Confederate general from Mississippi, Van Dorn, whose forces had been decimated trying to retake Corinth. Had Van Dorn been successful, he would then have marched on Nashville, thereby distracting the Federals in Kentucky and dividing their forces. Needless to say, Van Dorn never made it, and the Confederate advance became a retreat. The war in the west became that much more dangerous for Mississippi.[45]

Elder got more bad news the following morning. One of the Protestant boys enrolled in the bishop's school, Cathedral, was seriously injured when he fell out of a tree. Elder sent Father Grignon to go and check on the child.[46]

On Sunday, November 16, Bishop Elder allowed Father Finucane to deliver the homily. Finucane decided to preach on "learning to love God from all things we see around us."[47] This lesson must have been quite the challenge for Bishop Elder, his clergy and the people of Mississippi. Where was God in the midst of such profound grief and suffering?

Two days later, William Henry Elder noted in his diary that it was his parents' anniversary.

5
FLASHBACK: CHILDHOOD AND PARENTS

William Henry Elder had an idyllic childhood, and he was forever grateful to the parents who gave it to him. He made sure to always keep them a part of his life whether he was at seminary in Maryland or following his vocation in Rome.

Perhaps the greatest gift bestowed upon William Henry—or Billy, as he was affectionately called by his parents—was his Catholicism. His parents' piety and resoluteness in matters of faith is not surprising considering the family history. The Elders were amongst the first Catholic settlers in the colony of Maryland. They preserved that faith and handed it down through the generations in spite of violent anti-Catholicism. The young William Henry would have heard the story of his ancestor and namesake William Elder's defiant defense of his faith. When the Mass was outlawed in Maryland (except in private homes) in the early years of the eighteenth century, William built "a very large log house" two miles south of Emmitsburg, Maryland. He lived in one room but set aside the large hall to serve as a church lest any of the area's Catholics be deprived of hearing Mass. Little did William Elder know that his great-grandson William Henry would one day be put in a similar position.[48]

By all accounts, William Henry possessed a heightened sense of piety and devotion to his church from a very early age. By eighteen, he was contemplating entering a seminary. He wrote to his oldest sister, who herself had recently become a religious. (His parents had seven sons and three daughters and also took in several orphans and raised them as their own.)

Mount St. Mary's College in Emmitsburg, Maryland. *Library of Congress.*

William Henry wrote: "It has been, perhaps, three years since I began to make my vocation the subject of my prayers. For the last fifteen months I have remembered it almost daily in my supplications to Heaven, and since August last, I have made it the especial object of most of my Communions."[49] That same year, 1837, William Henry did indeed enter the seminary at Mount St. Mary's in Emmitsburg, Maryland.

From Mount St. Mary's, he wrote a letter further explaining his vacillation between the secular and religious worlds. He told his sister: "Many years ago, when I was very small, it used to be a favorite notion of mine, that I was destined to be a Priest. This early idea was most probably only the effect of the hopes I had sometimes heard expressed by Mother."[50] This revealing letter shows an eighteen-year-old's confusion and angst regarding his calling. He felt drawn to the priesthood, but something was holding him back, keeping him from making the final leap of faith. "If my own prayers and those, which I trust have been offered for me by you and the rest of our family, have had any immediate effect, it has been rather to confirm my early prejudice, and your fond hopes.... But it seems to me that I feel them, not so much in any better knowledge,

William Henry and his brothers. *Archives of the Diocese of Jackson.*

Archbishop Elder and his brothers

		Residence	Born
1.	Francis W. Elder	Baltimore, Md.	Sept. 16, 1807
2.	Basil T. Elder	Manhattan, Kans.	Feb. 14, 1811
3.	John C. Elder	Baton Rouge, La.	Feb. 23, 1813
4.	Joseph E. Elder	Chicago, Ill.	May 14, 1815
5.	Thomas S. Elder	New Orleans, La.	Feb. 4, 1817
6.	William H. Elder	Cincinnati, O.	Mar. 22, 1819
7.	Charles D. Elder	New Orleans, La.	Apr. 10, 1822

. . . .

This picture taken after Archbishop went to
Cincinnati at time of reception of Pallium.

. . . .

The Elder brothers. *Archives of the Diocese of Jackson.*

of the intention of Providence toward me....My final determination is yet to be made."[51]

Shortly after his agony on the Mount—the popular name for Mount St. Mary's—William Henry finally determined to enter the seminary. He quickly began to make his mark on the community and spent the years between 1842 and 1846 finalizing his training in Rome. He was ordained on Passion Sunday, 1846, by Monseigneur Brunelli.[52]

In 1846, Father William Henry Elder returned home to Maryland, where he began to live the Gospel that he preached.

The newly ordained priest served Emmitsburg and its vicinity for the next decade. He showed especial care to the marginalized, and his reputation for holiness became well-known. Among other acts of kindness, he was seen taking aid, temporal and spiritual, almost daily to an old black hermit who lived in isolation.[53] Such acts continued until William Henry was ordained bishop of Natchez and asked to leave his homeland in order to serve a de facto "diocese of the wilderness" more than a thousand miles away.

For Bishop Elder, 1862 was a lifetime removed from his younger, more pleasant days in Maryland. His world, and his nation's, had been turned upside down. Eight years earlier—on November 16, 1854—he had written to his parents from Mount St. Mary's to congratulate them on their anniversary. He concluded his devoted and loving letter: "Good bye, a happy anniversary and many happy returns of it. Pray for me, both of you, my dear Parents, and bless me, Your affectionate son."[54]

Now, in the gloom of 1862 Mississippi, the bishop yearned for the simpler days of a loving childhood. He yearned for the comfort and security his parents had always provided.

November 19, 1862, to February 23, 1863

The day after his parents' anniversary, Bishop Elder received good news: Frank Arrighi had returned home. Two days later, Arrighi himself, along with his sister Margaret, paid a visit to their bishop. Arrighi told Elder of the battle and showed him his wounded head.[55]

Death was again on Elder's mind when he attended Mass on Sunday. He allowed Father Grignon to preach, and the priest gave his homily on the Last Judgment. The rest of the week passed relatively uneventfully. Of course, there were a few reminders of the impermanence of life: some boys at the orphanage contracted smallpox, and the bishop received word that Father Mouton had finally received his official commission as hospital chaplain. Fear of another battle and its consequent suffering and death made Elder call up Father Georget from Biloxi to help out with the soldiers.[56]

The Advent season of 1862 began on Sunday, November 30. The bishop and his flock began to prepare for the coming of the Messiah. They also began to prepare for the inevitable Yankee invasion. From where it would come, no one knew—but come it would.

On the first Wednesday of Advent, Bishop Elder received a letter from Father Orlandi in Jackson pleading for a priest to be sent to the capital city, where soldiers were "dying in such numbers & in so many places." Elder promptly sent Father Finucane to assist Orlandi.[57]

The following morning, Elder lectured on Abel and Noah. Doubtless, he saw similarities in the fallen world around him: a fraternal strife in which the stronger smites the weaker, a sinful world consumed by death and destruction. Shortly after his lecture, Elder learned that one of his orphan boys, Biddy King, had died. Four days later, the bishop gave last rites to Catherine Kenny. Kenny had distanced herself from the Church for the past two decades, but now that she was at death's door, she eagerly reentered into communion with her native church. Elder was surely elated that Kenny's soul had been saved in time, but it would be one more earthly body that he would soon place into the ground and read the funeral rites over. There would be many, many funerals in the days to come.[58]

With Father Finucane gone in the direction of Jackson to aid the soldiers, Bishop Elder's duties multiplied. He began substitute teaching Latin on behalf of Father Finucane in addition to performing his normal episcopal duties. While the tedium of teaching—especially the monotony of teaching Latin—must have worn on Elder, he immediately saw the fruits of his manifold labors. The day after he became a full-time substitute, Bishop Elder was again called to Catherine Kenny's house. Although he had brought this stray sheep back into his fold the previous Sunday, the shepherd had one last duty to fulfill. Kenny rapidly deteriorated, and it was clear she would soon be dead. Elder gave her one final blessing and read to her the departing prayers. Immediately afterward, she became incoherent and faded in and out of consciousness. Five hours after her final blessing, Catherine Kenny was dead. Bishop Elder reflected on the great grace he had been a witness to:

> *It must have* [been] *especial prayers of her Mother in heaven,—that obtained for her to receive the Sacrts. just when she did.—What a happy thing is a good religious education. It kept the faith alive under all those cold embers of 25 years. And she had a distinct remembrance of the truths of her religion. She understood all about the Sacraments & the way to prepare for them. Blessed are the mysterious ways of God!*[59]

Bishop Elder finished his week with vigor and a new sense of purpose.

Oddly enough, Mr. Kenny, the husband of the recently deceased, returned to Natchez on Saturday and made his way to the bishop. The Protestant Mr. Kenny was furious at Elder's meddling with his wife's spirituality, and he let the bishop know it. That evening, Elder wrote: "In the afternoon Mr. Kenny came home very angry at his wife's reconciliation with the Church—scolded &c &c &c."[60] The bishop patiently bore the tongue-lashing, content that Catherine Kenny, at that very moment, was safely climbing the mountain of purgatory on her way to heaven.[61]

Later that night, Mr. Kenny was back at the rectory. If he was not contrite, he was at least accepting. He gave Elder permission to bury his wife in the church of her birth. Mr. Kenny even attended the funeral, though he stood in the back, near the door.

Bishop Elder himself presided over the controversial funeral. He spoke of Catherine Kenny's last request and emphasized her desire to receive last rites. The bishop proceeded to tell those present that her late reconciliation was not at all unusual. He explained "why people wished to die in the Cath. Church, because only there they have the helps & consolations wh. God has appointed—& taught in Holy Scrp. The Sacrts.—Penance—Eucharist—Extreme Unction—Communion of Saints."[62]

Elder buried Catherine Kenny, and he firmly believed that life went on—for Mr. Kenny, for himself and for Catherine Kenny.

That same day, the Kane family arrived after a thirty-five-mile journey from Louisiana. They asked Elder to baptize a seven-year-old girl and give first Communion and confirmation to a young man and woman who wished to seal their own baptismal promise by entering the church. Needless to say, Bishop Elder was delighted. Not often did he witness such devotion in the midst of such trial.[63]

Elder was even more impressed when the Kanes told him the story of a Catholic black man who lived two miles from them. The slave refused to work on Sundays, and his master beat him for it. These whippings happened several times, and still the slave refused to work on Sundays. When he learned that the Kanes were visiting Bishop Elder, the slave asked for a rosary and a crucifix. Elder sent this loyal son of Rome a rosary but had no available crucifix.[64] Throughout the war, Bishop Elder would minister to the martyred slave's brethren on the other side of the Mississippi River.

That same afternoon, the bishop baptized another child, offered catechism to others, heard confessions and, at night, offered yet another tutorial on the Holy Eucharist.[65]

Christmas gave Bishop Elder and his congregation a brief respite from the horrors of war. The bishop said Mass at 4:00 a.m. and again at 10:00 a.m., although he allowed Father Grignon to give the homily at the second Mass. With his spirits lifted, Elder hosted a small dinner party. Among the guests was General James Chalmers, who had been transferred to Natchez the previous Monday. After dinner, Elder and Father Guillou went for a ride to get some fresh air. It would be one of their final rides together.[66]

Bishop Elder wrapped up the Christmas season with some more Masses; a visit to the asylum (orphanage), which he enjoyed very much; and catching

Bishop William Henry Elder. *Archives of the Diocese of Jackson.*

up with Father Huber, who had recently returned from the Tenth Tennessee Regiment.[67] It seemed as if the winter season would prolong the stalemate between the opposing armies and allow the citizens of Mississippi a relatively peaceful couple of months.

D'Evereux Hall, Catholic orphanage for boys, Natchez, Mississippi. *Archives of the Diocese of Jackson.*

Then, on Tuesday, December 30, Bishop Elder received news that Vicksburg was again being attacked, and there was skirmishing at Port Hudson on the Louisiana side of the Mississippi River. "Expecting a general engagement at both places," and knowing the Creoles of Port Hudson had no priest, Elder immediately decided to visit them. (Elder allowed his priests to work outside his own diocese as freelance chaplains. He himself would sometimes cross the Mississippi River to Louisiana to render what aid he could, despite it being a separate diocese.) He sent Father Huber north to Vicksburg. It seemed as if not even winter could stop the bloody and destructive war between brothers.[68]

Elder left on New Year's Eve for Port Hudson and arrived there the following afternoon. Along the way, while waiting for his buggy to be repaired, Elder walked around the neighboring town of Bayou Sara. Later that night, Elder wrote in his diary, "walked through the burnt town, while the buggy was getting ready. Four blocks back from the river all burned— several fine brick houses—elegant gardens lying waste. All done by the Yankees last August."[69]

When he finally reached Port Hudson, Elder was greeted by Colonel Nelson A. Miles, leader of the famed Miles' Legion. The colonel greeted Elder kindly and offered him a bed in his own tent. Elder spent the rest of that day and the next hearing confessions in a borrowed tent. He took a tour of inspection the following day and saw the fortifications and batteries intended to keep the Yankees from taking the important fort. After getting a severe headache while touring the river defenses, Elder retired.[70]

The following morning, Elder again was hearing confessions and said Mass in front of the tent. A good number of the soldiers received Communion, which inevitably encouraged Elder to continue to offer his services as confessor. He did just that, spending Monday, Tuesday and Wednesday in the confessional/tent. The bishop realized that all this time hearing confessions was justified when he learned on Thursday night that one of the soldiers in the hospital had suddenly and unexpectedly died. Elder had heard his confession and given him Communion that Wednesday.[71]

The recently deceased Creole soldier was buried that same afternoon by Father Huber, who had just arrived with the Tenth Tennessee Regiment (he was again their chaplain). Unfortunately, Father Huber immediately fell sick with a sore throat and fever. Elder visited the sick priest on his way back to Mississippi.[72]

The return trip to his own diocese turned out to be quite an ordeal. Elder left Port Hudson during a heavy rainstorm. Because of high water, he could not return via Bayou Sara. Along the alternate route, his buggy passed through four lines of pickets only to find the creeks opposite Woodville, Mississippi, were also too high. Elder made the best of his time in Louisiana and heard more confessions. On Sunday, January 11, he was supposed to be celebrating the sacrament of confirmation with his Woodville parishioners. Instead, he heard more confessions in Jackson, Louisiana. He also offered Mass, gave a catechism class and prayed the rosary for the troops.[73]

On Monday, Bishop Elder, joined by Father Finucane, was able to make his way into Mississippi. With wet shoes—caused by having to leap from the buggy during the creek crossing—and suffering from diarrhea, Elder ate a small meal and got what sleep he could.[74]

He was up at eight o'clock the next morning saying Mass, teaching catechism and hearing confessions. He spent the next three rainy days doing the same thing, with an occasional baptism and confirmation. Father Finucane offered what help he could but was himself suffering from a bad cold.[75]

Elder left the sick Father Finucane and returned to Natchez on Saturday, January 17, 1863, after his seventeen-day trip into Louisiana and Woodville.

He came home to find Father Guillou in a very weak condition and heard via telegram that Father Huber had come down with a bad case of diarrhea.[76]

Over the next two weeks, Father Guillou rapidly deteriorated. On January 25, he and Bishop Elder went for a drive around town, but the priest was too weak to talk. Before they got back to the rectory, bishop and priest had to stop several times and rest before Guillou finally made it to his room. Ten days later, on February 4, it was clear that he was unlikely to survive much longer. Father Grignon moved into his room and kept watch over him throughout the night. Guillou survived the night and made his will the next day. Father Finucane then took a shift with his dying comrade until two o'clock in the morning, when Elder himself took over.[77]

Guillou survived yet another night. He spent the next day sitting in his chair giving "some fervent admonitions to those around him." His bishop and fellow priests prayed over him, and Elder gave him the viaticum—the final meal before his "passing over" to the next life—and last rites.[78]

Again, Father Guillou survived the night. Elder granted him a final absolution in anticipation of his imminent death. The tough priest lived another twelve hours, though he was in great pain and struggled mightily to breathe. He would gasp "for air for a quarter of an hour at a time." Finally,

Elder house, Natchez, June 1941. *Archives of the Diocese of Jackson.*

Natchez Cathedral, June 1940. *Archives of the Diocese of Jackson.*

at six o'clock that evening, Father Guillou's soul departed his consumption-ravaged body. Bishop Elder ran from the confessional to be with him in his final moments. The last thing Father Guillou heard was the ringing of the Angelus bells in the Cathedral.[79]

The pious of Natchez stopped what they were doing and prayed the prayer associated with the noonday bells:

> *And the angel of the Lord declared unto Mary.*
> *And she conceived by the power of the Holy Spirit.*
> *Hail Mary, full of grace…*
> *Behold I am the handmaid of the Lord.*
> *Let it be done to be according to your will.*
> *Hail Mary, full of grace…*
> *And the Word became flesh.*
> *And dwelt among us.*
> *Hail Mary, full of grace…*

Pray for us O Mother of God,
That we may be made worthy of the promises of Christ.

Pour forth, we beseech You, O Lord,
Your Grace into our hearts;
that as we have known the incarnation of Christ,
your Son by the message of an angel,
so by His passion and cross
we may be brought to the glory of His Resurrection.
Through the same Christ, our Lord. Amen.

The next day, Sunday, February 8, Bishop Elder celebrated Mass and exhorted his flock to practice acts of thanksgiving. No doubt, he himself gave thanks to God for the gift of his newly departed friend.

On Monday, Father Guillou was laid to rest. He was given a funeral worthy of a hero. The bishop processed in, then the acolytes, the schoolboys, the schoolgirls, the orphans, the nuns, the young Ladies' Society, the young Mens' Society of St. Aloysius and Father Guillou's brother priests. Then came the body of the beloved priest. Lastly, the congregation filled the church. The requiem Mass and funeral lasted nearly five hours.[80]

Exhausted, Elder still took the time to eulogize his friend in his diary:

Fr. Guillou's death is a sad calamity for the Diocese. Without injury to anyone—I can truly say he was the best missionary in the Diocese—so active, so zealous, so disinterested. He was also a favorite with all the other Priests—& a true friend & wise counselor for them—zealous also for his own perfection & for that of his Brother Priests. I feel as if his death was a judgement upon myself. God grant I may do better hereafter.[81]

The next several weeks passed as normally as war allows. The bishop said Mass, heard confessions and mourned his deceased friend.

The monotony changed on February 23, when the CSS *Queen of the West* sailed into Natchez.

7

THE *QUEEN OF THE WEST*

The CSS *Queen of the West* was not always the property of the Confederacy. In fact, it had once been the USS *Queen of the West*. The capture of the vessel was one of the very few Confederate naval successes of the war.

Near the beginning of the war, Charles Ellet had approached Secretary of War Edwin Stanton with a plan to win the riparian war in the west. Ellet designed a ship that proved ideal for fighting in the confined spaces of rivers. He sacrificed armaments and heavy guns for the sake of speed. Instead of traditional naval weapons, Ellet's ships would be fast steamships with large iron prows that would ram Confederate ships. Stanton was impressed, and he ordered nine such "Ellet Rams" to be constructed. The *Queen of the West* would be the flagship.[82]

The *Queen of the West* had an eventful—if not disappointing—history throughout the war. The ram first saw action on July 6, 1862, at Memphis, where it helped obliterate the Confederate Defense Fleet. Originally reported to be a "transportation vessel" by Confederate spies, it came steaming around a bend and made an immediate impact, ramming a more traditional Confederate ship. The *Queen*, was rammed in turn, and when Ellet came aboard to assess the damage, he was hit in the knee with a pistol ball. Weeks later, the inventor of the Ellet Ram was dead of infection. His prize, the *Queen of the West*, limped toward the Arkansas shore, having sunk a Confederate ship and helped prepare the capture of Memphis.[83]

Five weeks later, the *Queen* was repaired and fought one of the most odd and brazen naval battles of the war. It and a fellow ship attempted to sink the elusive and legendary Confederate ship *Arkansas*. Outdueled, the two Federal ships fled toward the Yazoo River, but the emboldened crew of the *Arkansas* pursued. In fact, the Confederate ship charged into the midst of ten to twelve Yankee gunboats and offered battle to all. After inflicting significant damage, the *Arkansas* escaped back downriver, where it avoided a second Union flotilla and docked safely under the guns of Vicksburg.[84]

Eight days later, on July 21, 1862, the *Queen of the West* aimed for redemption and, along with the ironclad *Essex*, once again tried to sink the *Arkansas*. Once again, the effort failed. This time, the *Queen* delivered a glancing blow but then ran aground. After maneuvering out of the mud, the *Queen* returned to the safety of the Federal fleet, mission unaccomplished.[85]

Six months later, on February 2, 1863, the *Queen* was ordered to sink the Confederate riverboat *City of Vicksburg*, which had recently brought much-needed supplies to Vicksburg and was now docked in plain sight of the Federal navy. Charles Rivers Ellet, the twenty-year-old nephew of the inventor of the Ellet Rams, surrounded his ram with double bales of cotton around his deck to fend off Confederate cannon shot. He then dawdled

Battleships and ironclads entering the Mississippi River. *Library of Congress.*

until day broke, and the *City of Vicksburg*—and Vicksburg itself—were on full alert. Furthermore, the *Queen* only managed a glancing blow on its target. It did, however, fire turpentine balls that caused *City of Vicksburg* to catch fire. Unfortunately for the *Queen*, the entire Vicksburg garrison opened fire on the clearly visible ship. Within minutes, the cotton bales were aflame, and the crew members were ordered above deck to push the defensive bales into the water. The *Queen* then fled to the Arkansas shore and the protection of its own batteries.[86]

Disappointed in the *Queen*'s repeated failures, the Federal commander sent it south with the easier task of raiding Confederate ships, which were moving supplies back and forth across the Mississippi River with near-impunity. Ellet's ram was far more successful on this mission, and the *Queen* captured a number of Confederate merchant vessels. But then, Ellet decided to sail eighty miles up the Red River in search of a rumored Confederate weapon. As he sailed between the banks, Rebel fire erupted all around him. Not long after, the *Queen* ran aground, and Ellet ordered his men to abandon ship. The *Queen* was quickly captured and converted into a Confederate ship. Fortunately for Ellet and his men, the Union sailors were rescued by the USS *Indianola*. The *Indianola* brought the rescued sailors back to the Federal fleet, then was ordered to return south and destroy the *Queen*, which was now a manned Confederate ram.

A view of Indianola, Mississippi, in 1860. *Yale University Library.*

Coincidentally, the now-Confederate *Queen* was presently under the command of Captain Hutton, who had attended St. Mary's College with Bishop Elder's brother Thomas.[87] The newest Confederate ship sailed into Natchez on February 23, 1863, and Bishop Elder treated the crew to some rare and valuable wine, then he and Father Grignon took an extensive tour of the *Queen*. The bishop walked away impressed and left a detailed description of the ram in his diary that night. The next day, the *Queen* sailed north and sank the *Indianola* in ten feet of water twenty-five miles south of Vicksburg. The *Indianola* was salvaged by Confederates and sailed south to join the few remaining Confederate ships on the Mississippi.[88]

Elder learned of the capture of the *Indianola* on February 26, 1863. Two days later, one of the soldiers who helped capture the *Indianola* paid his respects to Elder and informed the bishop that the ship had been destroyed by the Confederates in order to keep it from falling back into the hands of the Yankees. Something the informant neglected to mention to the bishop was the embarrassing cause of the destruction of the *Indianola*. The Federal commander, David Porter, had ordered a large flatboat to be extended and decorated with a paddle wheel, two smokestacks and a "Quaker gun" in order to make it resemble a large warship. The dummy boat was then christened *Black Terror* and sent drifting down the Mississippi River without a crew. Word quickly spread from Vicksburg to the crews trying to salvage the *Indianola* that a large Yankee warship was headed toward them, and the *Queen of the West* fled south. Rather than lose the *Indianola*, the Confederate salvage crew blew it up. Meanwhile, the *Black Terror* had beached itself on a sandbar.

February 25 to July 6, 1863

After the exciting events involving the *Queen of the West* and *Indianola*, Bishop Elder continued his usual yearly Lenten ministry. He instructed, heard confessions, said Mass and visited parishioners. Most notably, he said goodbye to Frank Arrighi, who left on March 3 to rejoin his company in Virginia. That same day, Elder received letters from Father Elia and Father Georget. The former was staying in Memphis, and the latter had returned to Biloxi too sick to continue his ministry among the soldiers in Jackson, Louisiana. Elder also learned that much of Holly Springs, Mississippi, had been burned.[89]

The tedium continued into the next week. Elder met with a disgruntled parent who threatened to take her children from the Catholic school. Bishop Elder and Father Finucane convinced her to keep them enrolled. Shortly after, a fire broke out in a nearby house, and Bishop Elder hurried to help extinguish the blaze. When the fire engine finally arrived, it broke down and had to be repaired. Finally, it entered the fray only to have the hose burst. When the fire was finally under control, Elder returned to the school to learn that two boys had wandered off at recess and never returned. One of his substitute teachers also wandered off the school grounds to watch the fire. The bishop later reflected: "Such a manifest want of judgement or ability coupled with the conversation of this morning disheartens me entirely."[90]

Elder spent the next three weeks filling his calendar with the same uneventful activities of a pastor: visiting parishioners, teaching, preaching, hearing confessions, consoling the sick. The bishop's life was truly one of delayed gratification. This was the life of nearly all Catholic pastors—the dullness of the ordinary. And yet, it was in doing the ordinary tasks that Elder's extraordinary character and constancy shone forth.

On March 27, 1863, Bishop Elder celebrated Mass. Confederate president Jefferson Davis had asked all Confederate churches to recognize this day as a day of supplication. Elder complied with Davis's request and said Mass at 10:00 a.m. and again at 7:30 p.m. He gave his first homily on the sorrows of the Blessed Virgin Mary. He reminded his suffering flock of the sufferings of their spiritual Mother and told them they must imitate Mary and bear their pains patiently. "For this momentary light affliction is producing for us an eternal weight of glory beyond all comparison" (2 Cor. 4:17).[91] His later homily centered around the words of St. Peter: "For to this you have been called, because Christ also suffered for you, leaving you an example that you should follow in his footsteps" (1 Peter 2:21). He begged his congregants to humble themselves and to see suffering as potentially meritorious. He exclaimed:

> We wish today to humble ourselves.…To accept our sufferings from God. Christ sees not the malice of men—but the decree of God for His own glory—& for men's happiness. So we must look beyond our enemies—to God's honor & our profit—winning us back from Sin.—We come to Rejoice in God's protection. Christ in His sorrows was filled with joy at the good that was to result.[92]

Elder concluded his homily and this national day of prayer by asking his congregation to remember the orphans, of which the war had created an abundance.

Incidentally, the collection that Friday was for the diocese's orphans. A Mr. Chiesa arrived that very day with three girls and two boys from Jackson who had recently been orphaned. There would inevitably be many, many more orphans thrown upon the mercy of Bishop Elder as the war raged on.

Holy Week went on in Elder's church as it had in the Catholic Church for the past 1,800-plus years. Natchez, Mississippi, celebrated the same feast days as Boston, Massachusetts; New York City; London; Hong Kong; Cairo, Egypt; and every other Catholic church across the globe: Palm Sunday, Tenebrae Wednesday, Maundy Thursday, Good Friday, Holy Saturday and, of course, Easter Sunday.

On that Holy Saturday, April 4, 1863, Bishop Elder said Mass. It was the anniversary of his own baptism, so no doubt, the bishop put all of his

A portrait of Jefferson Davis created by the Charles Daniel Feet Company. *Library of Congress.*

energies into his priestly duties that day. Afterward, he heard confessions for more than seven and a half hours.[93]

Easter Sunday in 1863 must have been difficult for the pious Catholics of the Diocese of Natchez. It must have been even more difficult for their shepherd. This day of rejoicing—the high point of the Church's calendar, the ultimate day of triumph—occurred in the midst of such unprecedented suffering. It must have seemed as if the people of Mississippi were permanently stuck in the sorrows of Good Friday. How could the people of the state relate to Resurrection Sunday?

Nevertheless, Bishop Elder summoned his inner reserves and preached the Easter homily. He told his congregation to rejoice with all those souls in limbo who had entered heaven this day. He spoke of how Satan's plans for earth had been ruined on Easter morn. He told them of the great battle in heaven in which Michael had cast down the usurper Lucifer and hurled him into hell, but the Evil One renewed the battle on earth, and his forces were plotting the ruination of God's earthly kingdom. But then, a little more than 1,800 years ago, Christ defiantly and definitively crushed the power of sin and death for the many. And yet this triumph of Christ, this victory over death, didn't come without its trials. Elder was trying to hammer home "the necessity of sufferings to gain the resurrection."[94]

The bishop was asked to put his homily into practice the next day, the Monday after Easter 1863. Elder's trusted friend and priest Father Finucane began spitting blood and experiencing sharp pains in his left chest. The doctor advised that he cease his teaching duties.

Elder had a replacement teacher in mind, but he worried that the young man would soon be conscripted. With classes set to resume soon, the bishop began to seek ways to hold onto his eager young teacher.

On the Thursday after Easter, Elder paid a visit to the orphanage and said Mass. Afterward, he dined with parishioners and catechized about twenty of their slaves. He was pleased with their devotion and knowledge of catechism.

When he returned home, Elder was delighted to find that Father Huber had arrived from Woodville and would soon be on his way to take over the parishes in Canton and Sulphur Springs.

The little spark of happiness that the orphans and slaves and Father Huber had given to Bishop Elder dissipated two days later, when he received a telegram from Father Orlandi: Father Basil Elia had died in Memphis eight days previous.[95]

It would only get worse for the bishop; Father Finucane again began, and then continued, to spit blood. Elder was worried that he would be forced to say yet another requiem Mass for one of his priests.

Instead, he would be offering prayers for the suddenly dead mayor of Natchez, John Hunter. Hunter had been a Catholic when he lived in Baltimore but had become a Methodist upon moving to Natchez. Elder had heard that the mayor was contemplating a return to his native religion. Unfortunately, he died suddenly while at work and never had the time to act on his intention.[96]

Days later, Elder rode up to Port Gibson, where he visited a number of parishioners. While in town, he admired the beauty of the newly finished Catholic church, St. Joseph. Luckily for the church and the town of Port Gibson itself, General Ulysses Grant would famously declare that the town was too beautiful to burn. St. Joseph would survive the war.

A portrait of Ulysses S. Grant created by John Chester Buttre. *Metropolitan Museum of Art.*

When Elder returned to Natchez on April 30, 1863, the town was in a state of panic on account of a successful Yankee cavalry raid that had crisscrossed the entire state of Mississippi. The citizens of Natchez feared the worst. Father Finucane had taken the precaution of moving the cathedral's valuables.[97]

Ten days later, Elder learned that the Federals had attacked Port Gibson on April 1, 1863. Fortunately, St. Joseph's accoutrements and silver had been hidden. However, the bishop soon learned that the preservation of the sanctuary's riches was of secondary importance, for one of his lambs, John Taylor Moore, was being hunted by Federal troops who intended to hang him.

Elder learned of Moore's fate on May 12. Moore had delayed the Federal assault upon Port Gibson by burning the suspension bridge leading into town. The Yankees planned to avenge this by capturing and hanging the rebel. Moore laid low for five days and then escaped into the countryside. Elder knew exactly where he was hiding and immediately set out to visit the fugitive. The bishop was warmly received and spoke at length with Moore about his escape. While there, Elder also learned that there were a fair number of Confederate troops wounded and dying in and around Port Gibson. Moore had no doubts that there were dying Catholics among them. Elder determined to set out the following morning for Port Gibson.[98]

Elder made the eighteen-mile trip to Port Gibson without incident and celebrated Mass at the absent Moore's house.[99] It was a convenient location, as all the church valuables had been secreted there. He spent the following days ministering to the wounded, who numbered about 180. Elder wrote of his horseback ride past the hospital to the battlefield:

> Some broken artillery wagons along the road & fragments of other things- wagons, boxes-haversacks-knapsacks-all torn however. I suppose everything serviceable has been picked up.-A great deal of torn writing paper scattered along:-a few carcasses of horses & mules. Two miles from town just at a little branch, behind a tree to the left was a body very badly buried: indeed not buried, but left lying on the surface, with some dirt thrown over it-& that so thinly that a hand or a portion of the arm was entirely exposed.-I was told that the Federals buried in this manner the most of our killed.-I mentioned it on my return, to the Mayor, Mr. Baldwin- & urged him to send some one to bury it properly.[100]

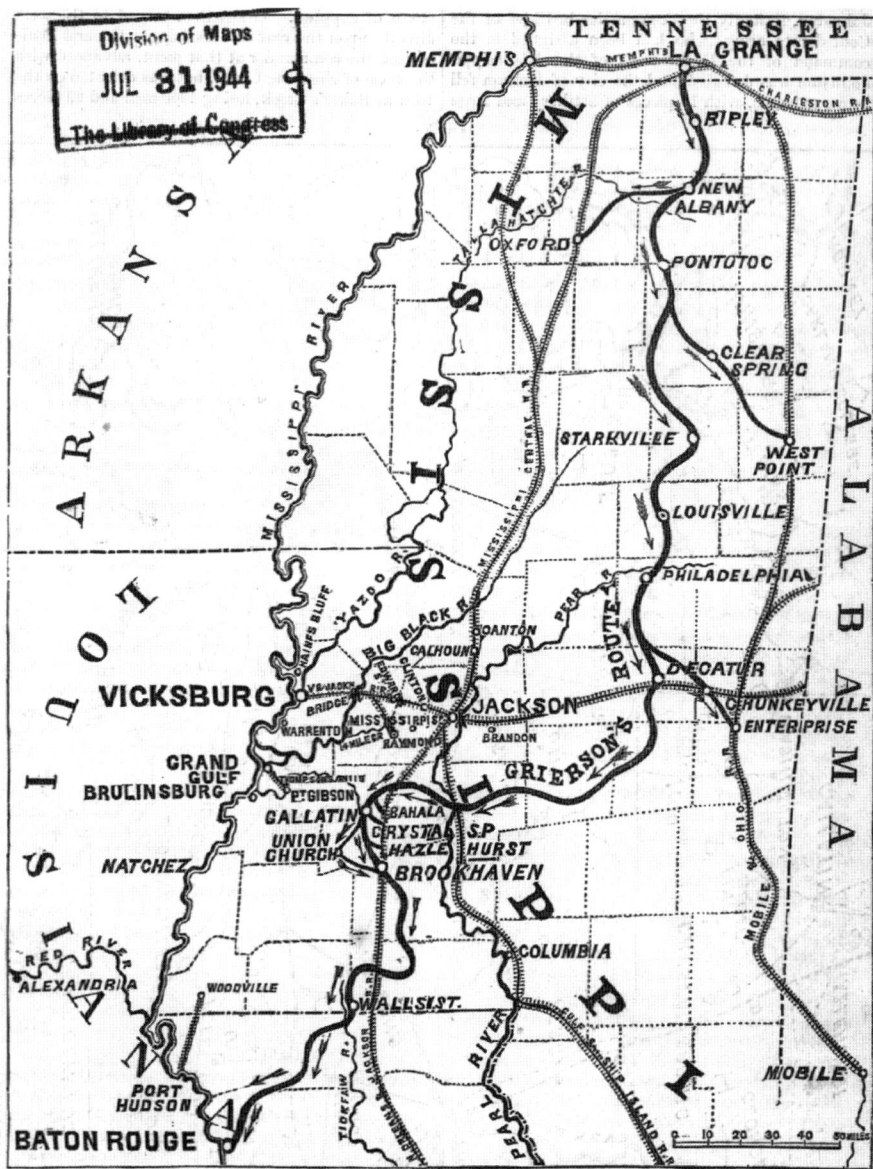

Colonel Benjamin Grierson's route from La Grange to Baton Rouge. *Library of Congress.*

After visiting with the wounded, Elder wandered across the battlefield. He walked through a house riddled with holes left by cannon shot and minié balls. As he left, two hounds who were lounging under the house came running toward him, begging to be caressed. The bishop complied. "They seemed lost for want [of] their master." But at least they were alive, unlike those in the newly dug graves Elder wandered past.[101]

Elder returned to Natchez on May 16 and, shortly after, learned that Jackson had been sacked. Unlike in Port Gibson, the church, St. Peter's, was burned to the ground. Within weeks, Federal gunboats were patrolling the Mississippi River with cannon aimed at the city—but the Federals had another target in mind.

MEANWHILE...IN VICKSBURG

The "Gibraltar of the West" became the nadir of hell for forty-seven days. From May 22 to July 3, 1863, Federal troops tightened their stranglehold on the city day by day and foot by foot. Unable to conquer the city by direct assault, General Ulysses S. Grant decided to starve the city into submission. But this siege was no mere waiting game. Grant ordered his cannons and sharpshooters to hurl in a continuous barrage of shell, shot and shrapnel. For forty-seven days, the Confederate soldiers suffered in the trenches. For forty-seven days, the civilians suffered in the caves they had been forced to dig and inhabit. For forty-seven days, Bishop Elder anxiously followed the developments of his diocese's second-largest city.

The story of the siege of Vicksburg has been covered exhaustively by scores of talented writers. But, perhaps the most moving accounts of the siege and the subsequent suffering were written by eyewitnesses Mary Webster Loughborough and Emily Balfour.

Loughborough and her husband, an officer in the Confederate army, were forced to flee their native Missouri at the outbreak of the war. A refugee, she followed her husband for the next two years and ended up in Vicksburg during the siege. (She also followed him to Oxford, Holly Springs, Jackson and Corinth.) She recorded notes in a diary during the siege that was immediately published in 1864 under the title *My Cave Life in Vicksburg*. It is a remarkable description of the sheer brutality of what was quickly becoming a staple of warfare: war brought directly to the people.

Right: Ulysses S. Grant statue, Vicksburg National Military Park, Vicksburg, Mississippi. *Library of Congress.*

Below: Map of the environs of Vicksburg, Mississippi, 1863. *Library of Congress.*

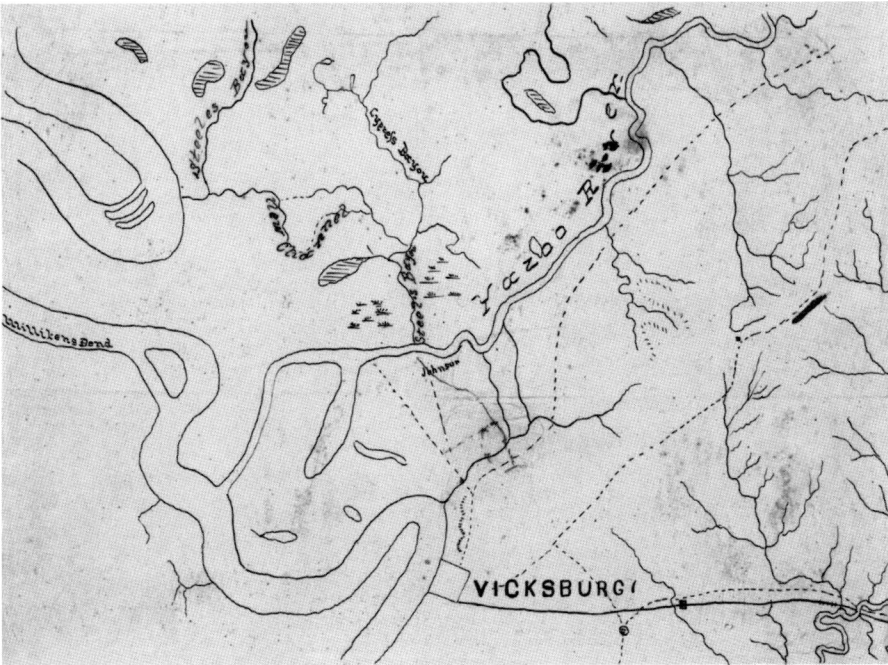

Emily Balfour was married to a wealthy doctor and owned one of the finer houses in Vicksburg. Consequently, she had an access to the movers and shakers of the siege that few others could boast. General John C. Pemberton was a frequent visitor and diner at her house, and Emily Balfour, unlike most citizens, spent the majority of the siege in her own home rather than fleeing to the caves. As a result, she was in constant contact with numerous Confederate officers.

The following are a handful of anecdotes recorded by Mary Loughborough and Emily Balfour. Their personal experiences are reflective of what the average citizen of Vicksburg suffered. Granted, Loughborough had some advantages not afforded to ordinary citizens—she was, after all, married to an officer—and Balfour had wealth and connections that few in Vicksburg could boast of, but their stories illustrate the pain and terror endured by all the inhabitants of Vicksburg, including those of Bishop Elder's own flock.

Early in the siege, Mary Loughborough witnessed the Federal fleet running by the Confederate batteries down the Mississippi River. Almost all of them made it—to the exasperation of the Confederate officers and citizens of Vicksburg. However, one transport was not so lucky and was hit by the rebel batteries. The boat burst into flames and continued to drift lifelessly after the more fortunate Union ships. Loughborough reflected on the death of the Federal sailors and on the mothers, wives and children who had lost their loved ones that night. She wrote, "Did this smooth, deceitful current of the glowing waters glide over forms loved and lost to the faithful ones at home? O mother and wife! ye will pray and smile on, until the terrible tidings come: 'Lost at Vicksburg!' Lost at Vicksburg! In how many a heart the name for years will lie like a brand!—lie until thwart heart and tired soul shall be at peace forever."[102]

Loughborough could not have made a more unfortunate understatement. The upcoming six weeks would create many, many more widows and orphans—most of them residents of Vicksburg and those fighting to defend the city.

Emily Balfour also witnessed the frequent duels between the Confederate batteries and the Union arsenal—gunboats and their own batteries dug into the Louisiana shoreline. She witnessed some of these confrontations from her balcony and sometimes from the spectacular view upon Sky Parlor Hill. The latter location contained a beautiful home owned by the Genella family, who were prominent Catholics. Their home could be accessed by traveling up a winding drive on the east side. The west side was a sheer cliff that provided an unobstructed view of the river. Many Vicksburg residents spent part of the siege taking in the glorious and deadly panorama.[103]

Shortly after the Federal boats slipped by the cannon of Vicksburg, the troops upon them, along with numerous shore batteries, began the systematic bombardment of Vicksburg that would continue for the next six weeks. Loughborough describes the effects of this bombardment:

> *My heart stood still as we would hear the reports from the guns, and the rushing and fearful sound of the shell as it came toward us. As it neared, the noise became more deafening; the air was full of the rushing sound; pains darted through my temples; my ears were full of the confusing noise; and, as it exploded, the report flashed through my head like an electric shock, leaving me in a quiet state of terror the most painful that I can imagine—cowering in a corner, holding my child to my heart—the only feeling of my life being the choking throbs of my heart, that rendered me almost breathless. As singly they fell short, or beyond the cave, I was aroused by a feeling of thankfulness that was of short duration. Again and again the terrible fright came over us in that night.[104]*

It is no wonder that the residents of Vicksburg, including Mary Loughborough, immediately began relocating to caves that they themselves dug into the sides of the city's numerous hills.

One of the unfortunate citizens who relocated to a cave home would grow up to become Mother Bernard McGuire of the Sisters of Mercy and the author of *The Story of the Sisters of Mercy in Mississippi, 1860–1930*. The future nun recalled: "At the first sound of warning my mother with her three children and a serving girl would arise and flee to the caves…I was seven. There was a sister of three and a baby brother 18 months old." She later remembered praying; battling rats, mice and mosquitoes; and dining on "marble size" potatoes and guarding a small piece of bacon as if it were the most valuable jewel.[105]

These new cave-homes provided shelter from the bulk of the shells and shrapnel fired into the city, but other dangers beset the refugees. Shortly after moving into her own cave, Loughborough was startled by loud, piercing screams. A black man had been buried alive in his cave not far from Loughborough's. The citizens frantically tried to dig him out, but by the time they reached him, he had already suffocated. "His wife and relations were distressed beyond measure, and filled the air with their cries and groans."[106]

Later, during the siege, Loughborough entered her cave to find a six-foot-long snake curled up in the supports of the roof. Fortunately, she saw it in time, and fortunately, her husband happened to be nearby and was able to stab it and sever its head.[107]

Cannon balls and their concomitant shrapnel sometimes found their way into the caves. One afternoon, a Federal battery began hurling Parrott shells in the direction of Loughborough's cave. She quickly called her slaves inside to take shelter. As soon as all were safely inside, another terrified man stepped inside her cave seeking shelter. All in the cave—Mary, her child, the slaves and the frightened guest—anxiously awaited the end of the barrage. However, one of the dreaded shells soon darted through the entrance and came to a stop in the center of the cave, still smoking. "Our eyes were fastened upon it, while we expected every moment the terrific explosion would ensue. I pressed my child closer to my heart, and drew nearer to the wall. Our fate seemed almost certain." They all stood, frozen with fear, looking at the "missile of death," when suddenly, one of the slave boys leapt to the center, grabbed the shell and hurled it to the other side of the street, thereby saving the occupants of the cave.[108]

Things would only get worse for Loughborough and her fellow citizens. The bombardment intensified as more and more began to seek shelter in the ever-growing number of caves. Unfortunately, those in the hospital did not have the option of hunkering down in a cave. When the hospital came under the same fire that plagued the rest of the city, the invalids could do nothing but pray. For some, the prayers worked, for one day, a shell went screaming through the hospital from end to end but miraculously hurt no one. Others were not so lucky. One already wounded soldier had his hip severely fractured by a cannon ball. Others were killed when a shell exploded in the hospital, sending deadly fragments into their wounded bodies.[109]

Emily Balfour recorded the events of Sunday morning, May 24: "Today a shocking thing occurred. In one of the hospitals where some wounded had just undergone operations, a shell exploded, & six men had to have limbs amputated. Some of them that had been taken off at the thigh, and one who had lost one arm had to have the other taken off. It is horrible, and the worst of it is we cannot help it."[110]

William Lovelace Foster, the Baptist chaplain of the Thirty-Fifth Mississippi Regiment, echoed Loughborough's and Balfour's horror at the condition of the hospital in letters home to his wife:

> There lay a man with most frightful countenance, scarcely human so much disfigured he was. His hair, eyebrows - eyelashes singed off - his face blackened - burned to a crisp with powder. His mother could not recognize him - Every feature was distorted....I behold a youth, not more than seventeen, lying on his back-with eye entering his jaw - lodging there in the bone, which could not be removed....Here are several with their arms cut - There is one with his whole underjaw torn off - his shoulder mutilated with a shell. Here is one with his arms - leg both amputated. What would life be to him if he could survive. There is one who had a pair of screw drivers driven into his jaw - temple. He floods his bed with blood. Why should I proceed any further? Every part of the body is pierced. All conceivable wounds are inflicted. The heart sickens at the sight....The weather is excessively hot -the flies swarm around the wounded....Never before did I have such an idea of the cruelty - the barbarism of war.[111]

In her book *Christ: The Living Water: The Catholic Church in Mississippi*, Cleta Ellington described the hospital during the siege:

> The whole air in the tents was contaminated. There lies one who had been mortally wounded—shot through the middle of his body. The flies swarm around him—he tears the bandage off. There is no hope for him. At last death comes to his relief. He was a Catholic.[112]

Not even children and babies were immune to the death-balls. Loughborough recalls three such deaths:

> Sitting in the cave one evening, I heard the most heart rendering screams and moans. I was told that a mother had taken a child into a cave about a hundred yards from us; and having laid it on it's little bed, as the poor woman believed, in safety, she took her seat near the entrance of the cave. A mortar shell came rushing through the air, and fell with much force, entering the earth above the sleeping child—cutting through into the cave—oh! most horrible sight to the mother—crushing in the upper part of the little sleeping head, and taking away the young innocent life without a look or word of passing love to be treasured in the mother's heart.
>
> I sat near the square of moonlight, silent and sorrowful, hearing the sobs and cries—hearing the moans of a mother for her dead child—the child that a few moments since lived to caress and love....The moans of pain came slowly and more indistinct, until all was silent; and the bereaved

mother slept, I hope—slept to find, on waking, a dull pressure of pain at her heart, and in the first collection of faculties will wonder what it is. Then her care for the child will return, and the new sorrow will again come to her—gone, forever gone![113]

A little negro child, playing in the yard, had found a shell; in rolling and turning it, had innocently pounded the fuse; the terrible explosion followed, showing, as the white cloud of smoke floated away, the mangled remains of a life that to the mother's heart had possessed all of beauty and joy.

A young girl, becoming weary in the confinement of the cave, hastily ran to the house in the interval that elapsed between the slowly falling shells. On returning, an explosion sounded near her—one wild scream, and she ran into her mother's presence, sinking like a wounded dove, the life blood flowing over the light summer dress in crimson ripples from a death-wound in her side, caused by the shell fragment.[114]

Even the household pets of Vicksburg suffered during the siege. Stray dogs had free reign in the city, and their bays and howls frightened Loughborough. She feared that hunger would drive the dogs mad and make them as dangerous as wolves. Yet, "[g]roundless was this anxiety, for in the course of a week or two they had almost disappeared."[115] Human hunger evidently triumphed.

The dead themselves could find no respite from the violence of the siege. The mounds of dead bodies quickly began emitting a collective repulsive stench. The smell became so overpowering that General Pemberton offered Ulysses Grant a truce so that he could bury the corpses. The Union general refused. Pemberton then offered to bury the Union dead himself. Again, Grant refused, and the bodies continued to bloat and broil under the summer sun.[116]

The gravity of the siege finally hit Emily Balfour like a thunderbolt when she saw several hundred mules being driven beyond the Confederate lines in the morning and another eight or nine hundred sharing their fate that evening. The exodus of the mules at first shocked Balfour, but then she realized the Confederate army did not have the food to feed its own livestock.[117]

Near the end of the siege, Mary Loughborough's young daughter grew sick and feverish. A Confederate soldier brought her a little jaybird as a gift to cheer her up. The little girl was delighted with her new pet and played with it as long as her fevered body allowed her. When she turned wearily away from the bird, one of Mary Loughborough's slaves turned to her and said, in a voice full of pity: "'Miss Mary…she's hungry; let me make her some soup from the bird.' At first I refused: the poor little plaything should not die; then,

INTERVIEW BETWEEN GRANT AND PEMBERTON.

Union general Ulysses S. Grant and Confederate general John C. Pemberton discussing the terms of the capitulation of Vicksburg, which led to the end of the Union siege of the city. *Library of Congress.*

as I thought of the child, I half consented. With the utmost haste, Cinth disappeared; and the next time she appeared, it was with a cup of soup, and a little plate, on which lay the white meat of the poor little bird."[118]

The ever reflective and pious Emily Balfour still found God in the midst of such unprecedented suffering:

> *In the midst of all this carnage & commotion, it is touching to see how every work of God save man, gives praise to him. The birds are singing as merrily as if all were well, rearing their little ones, teaching them to fly & fulfilling their part in nature's program as quietly & happily as if this fearful work of man was not in progress. The heavy firing gives us showers every day and nature is more lovely than usual. The flowers are in perfection, the air heavy with the perfume of cape jessamine & honeysuckle and the garden gay & bright with all the summer flowers. The fruit is coming to perfection, the apricots more abundant & more beautiful than I ever saw them. Nature is all fair and lovely—"all save the spirit of man seems divine."[119]*

Cave Life in Vicksburg during the Siege by Adalbert John Volck. *Metropolitan Museum of Art.*

Despite Emily Balfour's indomitable spirit, rations were reduced to starvation levels, and the psychological toll of the near continual barrage of shells and bullets, the piteous cries of the wounded and the heartsick wails over the dead finally convinced the citizens and soldiers of Vicksburg to put enough pressure on General Pemberton to ask for terms. He did, and the city of Vicksburg was handed over to Federal forces on July 4, 1863.

The cave of Mary Loughborough and her child is lost to history, just like the other hundreds of cave-homes made by desperate and fearful citizens. The home of Emily Balfour, however, would continue to play a role in Vicksburg's military occupation: it would become the headquarters of General James B. McPherson, the Federal commander of the District of Vicksburg from July 4, 1863, to March 1864. Bishop Elder would visit McPherson in the Balfour house in August 1863 to request that the Sisters of Mercy's convent in the city be returned to the nuns.[120]

Meanwhile, the suffering of tens of thousands of soldiers had finally come to an end. The sufferings of many of the residents was doomed to continue, as Bishop Elder would soon see for himself.

Sisters of Mercy arriving on the battlefield to succor the wounded after the Battle of Gravelotte, 1870. *Library of Congress.*

As an aside, because Natchez saw the futility of resistance, the city surrendered relatively early. Hence, the city was spared the destruction wrought upon Vicksburg and Jackson. The early capitulation ended up being a particularly fortunate boon for Natchez, for the city now relies heavily on the tourism industry. Many of its beautiful antebellum homes remain intact and draw thousands of visitors each year for the annual pilgrimages during which people can tour the old homes and gardens. Visitors can still see many extant antebellum homes, including Longwood, Stanton Hall, Rosalie, Concord Quarters, Sweet Auburn, Brandon Hall, Choctaw Hall, J.N. Stone House, the Gardens, the House on Ellicott Hill, the Coyle House, Pleasant Hill, Glenfield Plantation, Magnolia Hall, Williamsburg, Oak Hill, Lansdowne, Green Leaves, Hawthorne, Elms Court, Richmond, Shields Town House, Routhland, Linden, Airlie, Elgin, the Towers, Governor Holmes House and the Burn.

July 7 to July 20, 1863

Bishop Elder first heard rumors of the fall of Vicksburg on Tuesday, July 7, 1863. He and Father Rene Pont had left Natchez at 7:30 that morning on their way to Brookhaven. In light of their recent history, it must have been an awkward journey.

———

Father Rene Pont

In April 1861, Father Pont agreed to join the Confederate war effort as a chaplain when a number of his congregants enlisted in the Tenth Mississippi Regiment. Pont dutifully requested permission from Elder to follow the regiment outside the diocese to Pensacola, Florida. Elder reluctantly agreed but told Pont not to accept a commission—the bishop preferred his priests maintain a roving status so that they could attend to the needs of Catholic soldiers in a variety of units and not just the ones to which they were assigned. Somehow, whether through a misunderstanding or duplicity, Father Pont was appointed chaplain to Braxton Bragg's army on May 22, 1861. Elder gave Pont the benefit of the doubt, but when the priest later suggested that he remain with the army permanently, Elder gave him a piece of his mind: "You speak of looking on the camp as your home—& say that you told me before leaving there that Jackson was not your home any longer.—You are under some strange mistake in that respect.—I never thought once of depriving the Diocese permanently of a Missionary….If you have any other views now, I am glad to correct them at once."[121]

Not long after he learned of his superior's frustration with him, Father Pont was with the Confederate army at the Battle of Shiloh and its aftermath. Just before twenty-four thousand persons lay dead, dying and wounded on that field, the priest had reported to his bishop that there were about ten thousand Catholics in the area preparing for battle and only three priests—two that spoke only French and himself.

Father Pont ministered to the wounded and accompanied the army back to Corinth. He escorted more of the wounded to Vicksburg, where he learned that he was needed back in his native France. He promptly left to handle the family business and did not return for a year.[122]

On Saturday, May 16, 1863, Elder returned to Natchez from Port Gibson, where he had been performing ministerial duties and visiting the wounded. To his delight, he found Father Pont waiting for him. The two caught up on happenings in France and New Orleans.

A week after their reunion, Elder learned of the destruction of Jackson, and about six weeks later, Elder and Father Pont began their journey to the capital. They traveled thirty-two miles that first day and stayed the night at an acquaintance's. The next morning, they were on the road by 5:30 and made it to Brookhaven ten and a half hours later. In Brookhaven, the bishop met up with Father Picherit and heard the propitious news that Vicksburg remained in Confederate hands. Elder, Pont and Picherit were together for only a brief time. That same afternoon, Father Pont caught a ride to Monticello, Mississippi, and boarded a skiff on which he sailed down the Pearl River to Pass Christian. Father Pont would spend the rest of the war in the normally quiet coastal town.

———

On July 9, Bishop Elder again started early, this time for Jackson. However, he was stopped at Hazlehurst and turned back by order of Confederate general Joseph E. Johnston. Elder spent the next four days in Brookhaven.[123]

The bishop was pleased with the progress of the sleepy little town. Just two years earlier, Father Picherit was living in a house that doubled as the

Father Henry Picherit. *Archives of the Diocese of Jackson.*

General Joseph E. Johnston. *Library of Congress.*

congregation's church. The priest slept in the back room, while the front was reserved for Mass and the sacraments. The Brookhaven church's first baptism was performed in Father Picherit's house-church in November 1861, when he baptized Rosa Grant, the daughter of Patrick and Mary Grant.

The Catholics of Brookhaven built the area's first church in the midst of the war in 1863. The Grant family—mother, father, three daughters and two sons—lived next door to the new church. Interestingly, the three daughters remained spinsters until their death, and the two brothers remained bachelors. Thus died out the Patrick Grants of Brookhaven. As Bishop Elder was soon to learn, many other Catholic and Mississippi families would suffer the same fate—though not by choice.[124]

With the fate of Vicksburg still uncertain, Elder said Mass in the new and nearly finished church that had been built by Father Picherit and his congregation. The bishop and priest decided that the new forty-by-twenty-foot church would be dedicated to St. Francis of Assisi. Perhaps the desire for the patronage of the patron saint of peace reflected each man's longing for peace in their own time, in their own land. Sometime that day, Elder received definitive word that Vicksburg had fallen.[125]

The bishop was back in the church at 4:00 p.m. for the recitation of the rosary and to confirm five new Catholics. No doubt, the suffering and death of so many in Vicksburg was on the bishop's mind. He must have been happy to add these five new Catholics to his diocese, for there was no telling how many had lost their lives during the siege.[126]

On Tuesday, Elder again tried to reach Jackson. However, the road just beyond Crystal Springs was washed out, and he was forced to turn around and spend the night in Crystal Springs. He was forced to cut a deal with one of the locals—the man would carry the bishop's traveling bag in his wagon while Elder rode the man's horse. The bishop coughed up an exorbitant twenty-five dollars to cover the thirty-five miles to Brandon. That same day, the bishop met some paroled Confederate prisoners from Vicksburg and mailed a letter to his brother, Francis, in Baltimore.[127]

The following morning, Wednesday, July 15, Elder set out for Brandon. He was forced to take off his overcoat, fold it and place it on the saddle, which was too rough to sit on. On the way, he met some more paroled prisoners from Vicksburg. The bishop dismounted and let one of the sick parolees ride for a while as he walked alongside the horse he had just rented for twenty-five dollars. It was during this walk that he first learned of the horrors that attended the siege in Vicksburg. The men had been in the trenches for forty-seven days and had been reduced to quarter rations; even the mules were slaughtered and served to the hungry soldiers. This report was only a preface to the sufferings the bishop would soon hear about in regard to the siege. Elder immediately visited the hospitals in Brandon but, fortunately, did not have to perform last rites.[128]

The following morning, Father John Bannon of Missouri paid his respects to Elder, reported on events in Vicksburg and took his leave to follow the army eastward. (Shortly after, Father Bannon would be sent by the Confederate government to his native Ireland to try to halt the increasing number of Irish men who immigrated to the United States and found themselves in Yankee uniforms—as many as 150,000, including those already in the United States at the start of the war.[129] Bannon was not too successful and spent the remainder of the war, and his life, as a Jesuit in Ireland.) Elder was also visited by the owner of his rented horse, who delivered his traveling bag to him. Perhaps still chagrined by the $25, Elder decided to buy his own conveyance. Between visiting the hospital and shopping for reliable transportation, the day flew by. It ended with the bishop in possession of a new horse and buggy—at a cost of $1,000. It was a steep price, and Elder blamed the depreciated Confederate currency. The ever-thrifty bishop eased his conscience by reassuring himself that he could sell them in Natchez for the same price if necessary. He also realized that there simply was no way into Jackson—no one would lease horses for fear of impressment. In short, Elder had no choice but to make the investment.[130]

The bishop spent the next day in Brandon and witnessed the retreat of General Johnston's Confederate army. Elder understood that this retreat meant that Jackson, his destination, was now—or soon would be—in Federal hands.[131]

The following morning, Saturday, July 18, Elder finally made his way to Jackson. At first, the Confederate commander of the rear guard refused to let him pass. When the bishop explained that he intended to visit the Sisters of Mercy and their field hospital, he was allowed to proceed. And proceed he did, past stragglers, debris and bale after bale of burning cotton, until he came upon Federal pickets who, like the Confederate rear guard, also challenged him. And like the Confederates, they also let him pass. The bishop made his way to the rebel field hospital now under the charge of a doctor from Elder's home state of Maryland.[132]

Elder was shocked to see that not only had the nuns departed for Lauderdale Springs, Mississippi, but there was also no priest to attend the wounded and dying. He himself performed that function. He found an expiring soldier who had been shot through the head and gave him last rites.

The Battle of Jackson. *Library of Congress.*

Elder offered what consolation he could until nine o'clock in the evening, when he took supper and retired to an abandoned tent.[133]

Bishop Elder spent the next day, Sunday, visiting the field hospital. The wounded and captured (but recently abandoned/released) Federal soldiers were moved to Jackson proper. Elder still had plenty of work to do in the hospital—so much so that he wasn't able to celebrate Mass.[134]

The following morning, he again ministered to the unfortunates in the hospital. After lunch, he finally made his way into the conquered capital. The damage he saw from Brandon to the outskirts of the capital city paled in comparison to what he now saw. He drove by burning buildings, ruined rail tracks and "warm ashes—& ruins at every step. Melancholy desolation."[135] Far worse awaited the bishop inside the city itself. When he saw the remains of so many houses and businesses of which only the masonry chimneys remained, Elder quickly understood the reason for the capital's new sobriquet: Chimneyville.

11

St. Peter's Becomes a Relic of "Chimneyville"

On May 16, 1863, Father Orlandi rushed up to the commanding Federal officer and pleaded with him to not set fire to the barrels of tar he had just moved to the middle of the street. Father Orlandi's church, St. Peter's, was just on the other side of the street and would certainly be engulfed in the flames. The officer ignored the pleas of the priest. Union surgeon Dr. H.S. Hewitt intervened and echoed the priest's request. Again, the officer refused to acquiesce. According to Sister Mary Ignatius Sumner of the Sisters of Mercy, who was near St. Peter's when this exchange occurred, the water hoses had already been slashed and, incidentally, the Irish Catholic troops had already been sent back to their bivouac when the order came to burn the church. Once the flames began, they would rage until they were satiated.[136]

After fifteen minutes of Father Orlandi and others requesting, pleading and begging, St. Peter's church was in flames, along with the buildings surrounding it, including the school and presbytery, where Father Orlandi lived. Just before it was set aflame, Fathers Orlandi and Leray, along with Dr. Hewitt, went inside and removed the Host and wine, ornaments and furniture.[137] Father Leray approached and told the Federal officer: "You would not dare to insult me, but that you know my office prevents resentment."[138]

Sister Sumner, who served all over Mississippi during the war, noted that after the burning of St. Peter's, Dr. Hewitt went back to Vicksburg and established his offices in St. Paul's Church. She suggests he did so in order to keep another Catholic church from going up in flames.[139]

Within a week, the Catholics of Jackson, with the help of the Sisters of Mercy, had constructed a new building in which to celebrate Mass. One week later, General William Tecumseh Sherman was back and ready to put his fire-and-brimstone theory of war to the test. Sherman believed the war would go on and on, at the cost of more and more lives. His time in Louisiana as headmaster of the Louisiana State Seminary and Military Academy (later Louisiana State University) had convinced Sherman of the toughness and ferocious devotion of the average white Southerner to the cause. Unlike many Northern generals and politicians, Sherman knew the war would be long and bloody. In hopes of shortening it, he urged his commanders to bring the war to the people. Make those on the home front feel the effects of secession. Make them put pressure on their husbands, fathers and sons to end the killing, and make those husbands, fathers and sons so concerned for their family's welfare that they become distracted Confederate soldiers—and perhaps even deserters.

Thus, Jackson was burned—for the first time.

GENERAL GRANT AND HIS STAFF ENTERING JACKSON, MISSISSIPPI.

Ulysses S. Grant rides into Jackson. *Library of Congress.*

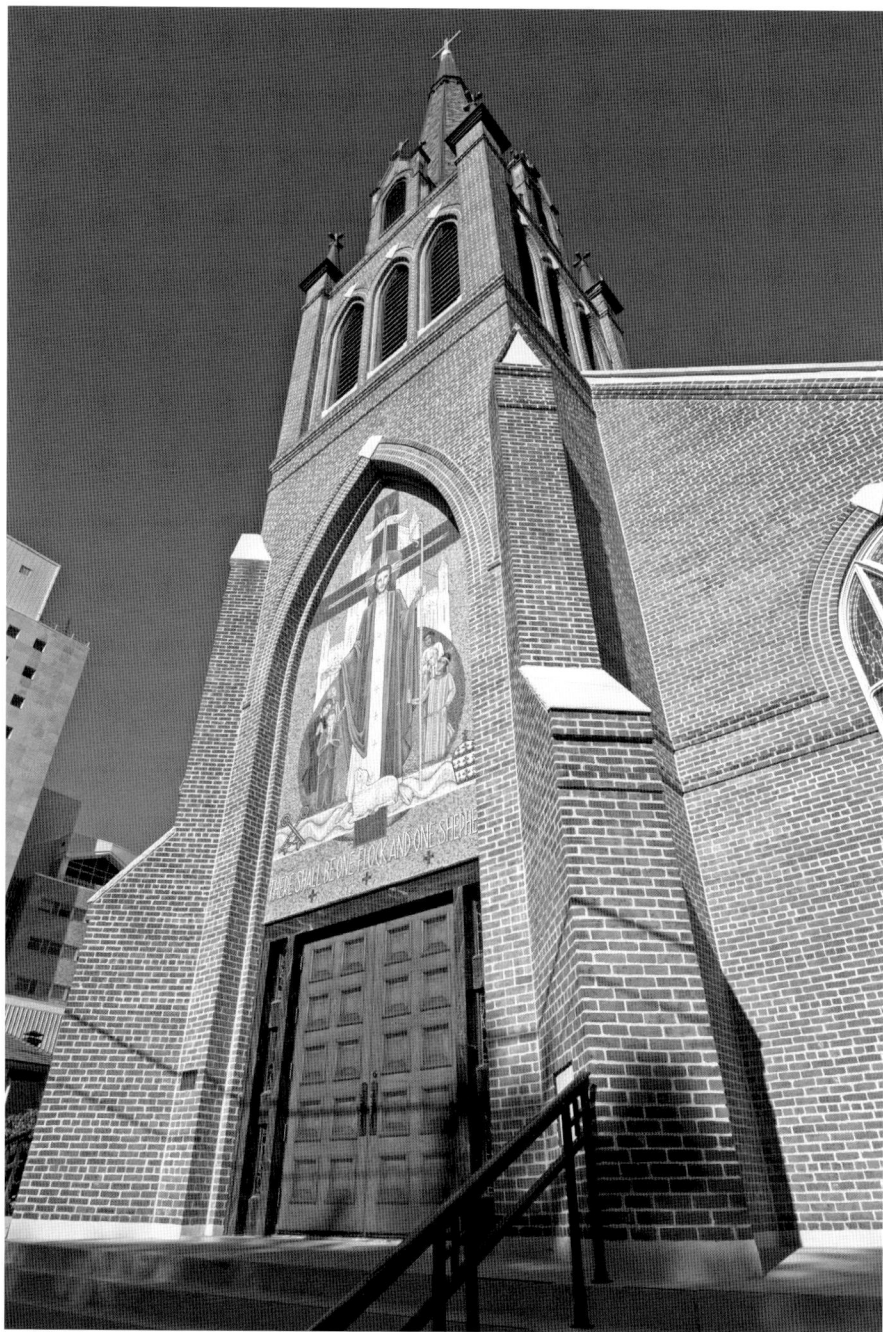

St. Peter's Church, 2018. *Josh Foreman.*

A week after the parishioners of St. Peter's celebrated Mass in their impromptu hall-turned-church, it, too, was burned to the ground. This time, the furniture and ornaments were not spared. Union soldiers looted the church and made off with the vessels. They did, however, leave behind a smashed crucifix.[140]

The church was rebuilt and relocated but was taken over by the Federals in 1864. Two valuable statues were destroyed, and the altar was used as a butcher's block.[141] Father Orlandi personally visited General Grant to request compensation for the damaged property of an institution that could not have been a legitimate war target. Grant denied the request.[142]

A crestfallen Father Orlandi requested that Bishop Elder allow him to return home to Italy. Elder gave his permission to the unhappy and broken priest. Orlandi boarded a boat for his native land. He never returned to the United States, the land he had called home for six years.[143]

12

July 20 to July 24, 1863

As of July 20, 1863, Father Orlandi's future was as yet undetermined. That evening, Father Orlandi met Bishop Elder at a parishioner's house. There, Elder learned that the temporary chapel built to replace the already burned St. Peter's had also been burned. The chapel's crucifix and chalice had been stolen. Fortunately, a Catholic Union soldier saw his compatriots drinking from it later that evening and bought it from them. He immediately returned it, chipped and damaged, to Father Orlandi.[144]

Father Orlandi's house was not as fortunate. The Union soldiers ransacked it and stole all of his clothes and food. The priest was given army rations, but without a place of his own, he had no way to cook them. The night he reported the destruction of the chapel, he had eaten only crackers.[145]

That same day, Bishop Elder prudently sought out General Charles Ewing, a Catholic Yankee. The general agreed to shelter Elder's horse and buggy and to make sure that the Sisters of Mercy's convent was left unscathed. In spite of Ewing's kindness, the bishop had difficulty getting through the meeting. "I [could] not talk much. I felt myself choak [sic] with sadness & indignation."[146]

After meeting with the "kind" and accommodating General Ewing, Elder and the Union priest, Father Joseph C. Carrier of the Sixth Missouri, went to Union general F. Blain to obtain a pass to go to Canton.[147] Blaine reluctantly gave the pass to the bishop. Father Carrier then invited Elder to dine with him and General Ewing. The bishop refused for fear of how insensitive it would look to his suffering parishioners. He also refused to say Mass in the

Vicksburg convent of the Sisters of Mercy. *Archives of the Diocese of Jackson.*

now-conquered and occupied Senate Chamber for the same reason. Instead, he went straight to Canton. Unfortunately, it took the bishop hours to get out of the city due to the destruction. No doubt, his frustration increased when Father Orlandi informed him that he could buy a good horse and buggy for only $25 in Federal money (as opposed to the $1,000 Confederate specie he had just spent to purchase a horse and buggy in Brandon). Elder made it fifteen miles outside of Jackson when rain forced him to seek shelter just five miles outside of Canton.[148]

Elder reached Canton at 9:30 the following morning. He was greeted by Father Huber, who was staying at a comfortable house recently evacuated by a parishioner. When the Union troops approached the house four days earlier, Father Huber greeted them kindly and was able to save the house and provisions. A fellow parishioner, Nancy Luckett, was not so fortunate. The Federals made away with all her food, horses, mules and carriages.[149] Elder offered his condolences and moved on to Mrs. Thomas Semmes's house for the evening.

Interestingly, this episode was not the Lucketts' first run-in with the authorities. Eight years prior, another of the Madison County Lucketts,

Oliver Luckett, had hosted Elder's predecessor, Bishop James Oliver Van de Velde. The fifty-nine-year-old and fragile Van de Velde was accompanying five sisters from Vicksburg to Canton in a stagecoach. The nuns were going to run the new school in Sulphur Springs. The owner of the stagecoach happened to be a member of the Know-Nothing Party, an anti-Catholic political party that had recently made its presence felt in Mississippi. Rather than ride outside the carriage with the driver, as was his custom, the owner decided to sit inside with the bishop and nuns. It soon became clear to Van de Velde that the man was drunk. In fact, he was *very* drunk—and belligerently drunk at that. On the road to Canton, the man suddenly exclaimed: "You know what, I think you are a priest! So take that!" as he projected a stream of tobacco into the bishop's face. Van de Velde calmly wiped his face, only to have the owner repeat the shenanigan each time he needed to spit. By the time the party reached Canton, the bishop had deflected several streams of saliva-tobacco with his hat. When the coach finally stopped to change horses, Bishop Van de Velde rose to his diminutive height, grabbed the offending owner and hurled the man from his own coach. The rest of the journey proceeded without incident.[150]

When the bishop and nuns disembarked at Canton, they were met by Judge Oliver Luckett, who took them to his house. While there, Luckett expressed his concern to Van de Velde regarding the Know-Nothing Party.

Bishop James Oliver Van de Velde. *Archives of the Diocese of Jackson.*

He was worried that if his fellow Cantonites learned that he was boarding a Catholic bishop along with five sisters, he would be in dire straits. Fortunately, the night passed without incident, and the bishop and his nuns were on their way to Sulphur Springs in the morning; interestingly, they traveled in the care of Dr. Alphonsus Semmes,[151] a relative of the woman who was now boarding Van de Velde's successor.

On Thursday, July 23, Bishop Elder intended to say Mass in Mrs. Semmes's dining room but found this to be impossible. So many refugees had fled to the Semmes house that the dining room had become a dormitory. Instead, the bishop said Mass in a rough outdoor shed. Despite the shoddy altar, Mrs. Semmes begged Elder to allow Father Huber to say Mass three Sundays a month instead of his previously arranged two. If he did, the Catholic community would raise his pay from $350 to $500. Mrs. Semmes must have been a pragmatist, for she assured the bishop that if the Confederate currency should fail, as must have seemed likely at that point, she would see to it that Father Huber was at least housed, fed and clothed. This promise of food and care must have been music to the ears of Father Huber, who had been suffering from frequent attacks of diarrhea.[152]

After making arrangements for the health of his priest, the bishop traveled to Madison to visit his friend Dr. Michael O'Reilly. His visit lasted for more than two hours on account of a storm that delayed Elder's departure. It must have been an uncomfortable afternoon for the bishop, for he later wrote: "[T]he good doctor much out of spirits."[153] Although O'Reilly's house was still intact, all of his slaves were leaving him. With Federal troops so close, there was nothing he could do to keep them on his homestead. Elder listened to the doctor's complaints but didn't have any practical advice. When the storm finally passed, Elder was on his way back to Canton.

The day proved productive but somber. When the bishop arrived in Canton, he went straight to another acquaintance's house but found it full of paroled Confederate soldiers. He continued on to yet another friend's house, where he finally found a meal and rest for the night when the already-sleeping owner awoke and welcomed him in.[154]

Elder was up early the next morning—early enough to announce to the Catholic community that he would be saying Mass at 7:00 a.m. Unfortunately, the bishop did not bring the appropriate altar bread, nor could he procure any on such short notice. Instead, he said the Litany of the Saints for the parishioners. Afterward, he dined, then visited a few members of his flock. Then, the bishop began what was a very difficult task for him—the settling of his dear friend Father Guillou's effects.[155]

13
THE BATTLE

The date was September 17, 1862. The 228 remaining men of the Sixteenth Mississippi Regiment marched toward the sound of battle. Shell, grapeshot, canister shot and small-arms fire whizzed by them, around them and sometimes through them. Yet, the men of the Sixteenth Mississippi held their ground until they were ordered to retire. Unfortunately, receiving that "destructive fire" and returning it as best they could was just the beginning of a long, bloody day for the regiment. It was still only ten o'clock in the morning.

After their withdrawal, the men were ordered to counterattack. They did. Again, they were caught in the midst of a murderous fire—this time, a crossfire between two enemy batteries. Again, they withdrew as orderly as before. For the next hour, the men of the Sixteenth Mississippi endured a constant barrage from Federal shell and solid shot. Thinking they finally had the Mississippians whipped, the Yankee commanders ordered their own charge to mop up what remained of the Sixteenth. The Federals moved out en masse between four and five o'clock in the evening. The Sixteenth rose once again and marched out to meet them. This time, it was the Federals who broke and ran. The men of the Sixteenth returned to their positions, grateful for nightfall.

The official report from the Battle of Sharpsburg filed by the commander of the Sixteenth Mississippi, Captain A.M. Feltus, read: "The number of men carried into the action was 228; of them, 144 were killed or wounded, leaving only 84 men."[156]

Union army troops at Antietam. Group at Secret Service Department, headquarters, Army of the Potomac, Antietam, October 1862, by Alexander Gardner. *Metropolitan Museum of Art.*

Now, it was Father Ghislain Boheme's turn to get to work, for there were many needing consolation, medical care and last rites. But Father Boheme never came to the men he had campaigned with for the previous two months—he was already dead.

Death Comes to the Beloved Priest

Father Ghislain Boheme was one of Elder's most able missionary-priests. The Belgian-born priest had arrived in Natchez twenty years before the war. At the time, Mississippi was still a frontier, and the foreign priest was often the sole pastor of all of east Mississippi and west Alabama. His circuit rides took him into both states and from the Gulf of Mexico to Tennessee. "In numerous Catholic families scattered over that vast expanse it was this missionary priest on horseback who kept the faith alive and who made it known and respected by all who met him, not a few of whom he had the happiness of receiving into the Church."[157]

Father Boheme began his final earthly odyssey when he boarded a train in Mississippi to join the Sixteenth Mississippi Regiment in Virginia. Although he never served as an official Confederate chaplain, and records of his final two months are scarce, it is easy to piece together his activities from April 25, 1862, until his death on June 27, 1862. A fair number of soldiers in the Sixteenth left behind detailed diaries, journals and letters regarding their adventures. Father Boheme left no such record, but his comrades have left behind a vivid impression of life in the Sixteenth Mississippi Regiment.

The day Father Boheme left Mississippi, it snowed in Virginia. In fact, it snowed a lot—three to four inches. When the train bearing the priest arrived, it was raining. Needless to say, it was an inauspicious start to Father Boheme's final days.[158]

The priest received a very quick—and likely alarming—introduction to army life. The soldiers' daily rations consisted of raw meat and parched corn. Upon such a diet, they were sometimes required to march as many as thirty-one miles in a day.[159] Immediately upon Boheme's arrival, the meat ration was cut from twelve to eight ounces.[160] The fifty-nine-year-old priest tightened his belt and joined the ranks.

The real challenge for Boheme began a week after he arrived. The troops were told to break camp—they would soon be engaging the enemy. However, where and when and which enemy's armies they would face remained a mystery. Captain Jesse Ruebel Kirkland wrote home to his wife, Lucinda, in Mississippi: "Everything is kept in the dark. We know not who to trust, as so many of our movements have been telegraphed to the world. We are kept on the move all the time." Little did Captain Kirkland, or any of his fellow Mississippians of the Sixteenth, know that they were about to embark upon one of the most daring, trying, successful and epic campaigns in military history.[161]

After one week of marching, James Johnson Kirkpatrick of the Sixteenth wrote in his diary on May 15, 1862: "Started on the march today at ten o'clock. Commenced raining soon after and continued all day. Marched fifteen or eighteen miles which, considering the rain and want of rations, was as much as we were able to do. Halted shortly after dark."[162] Such a pace, coupled with the weather, took its toll on the regiment. Franklin Lafayette Riley noticed the increasing number of sick. "Sam Walker (B) died May 15 at Charlottesville (of Typhoid). The regiment has lost another 35 men, 16 from deaths in hospitals since April 29."[163] Clearly, Father Boheme was kept busy from the moment of his arrival.

The next day, the Sixteenth Mississippi Regiment was assigned to General Thomas "Stonewall" Jackson's Second Corps of the Army of Northern Virginia. They were about to embark on a forty-eight-day, 646-mile, skirmish-after-skirmish, battle-after battle campaign that would immortalize them in the annals of military history. Jackson's daring campaign would prevent two Union armies from joining forces and capturing Richmond, thereby ensuring that the Confederacy would live to fight another day, although, of course, it was ultimately defeated.

Kirkpatrick wrote in his diary: "Saw 'Old Jackson' today for the first time. He was stopped at a house and came out, by request, as we passed

An unidentified Confederate veteran, Rojas & Conner. *Library of Congress.*

by. The Sixteenth gave him a good cheer. He was clad in an old sunburnt coat and cap."[164]

Two days later, on May 23, 1862, Stonewall Jackson led his troops in the Battle of Fort Royal. It was a harbinger of things to come—at least, for the near future. The Sixteenth Mississippi suffered no casualties, and the Confederate army took five to six hundred prisoners. "Everyone," according to Kirkpatrick, "[was] in high spirits."[165]

The joy of victory and the adrenaline of battle lust continued the next day, when the rebels chased after the fleeing enemy. Then, the reality of army life hit. Kirkpatrick, who had been so ecstatic the day before, recorded in his diary: "Slept on our arms tonight and came very near freezing. We had neither coats nor blankets…and the night is exceedingly cold." The Sixteenth was "in motion by daylight," and the euphoria of the previous day returned as they pursued the Federals for eight miles.[166]

The cold night was long forgotten as the Sixteenth Mississippi Regiment basked in the glory of victory. Their collective spirit rose even higher when the official battle reports came out. Confederate general Isaac R. Trimble credited the activity of the Sixteenth with winning the battle. He wrote: "This movement [positioning themselves to flank the Federals]…no doubt had an immediate influence in deciding the result of the day."[167]

Glorious battles and heady recognition soon gave way to the humdrum of marching, pitching tents, breaking down tents, more marching and the countless daily tasks necessary for camp life in the army. The day after the battle, Franklin Lafayette Riley wrote in his diary:

> *Picket duty.…At Divine Service (4 P.M.) Chaplain Reeves preached. I don't know the subject of his sermon. I was there, but I was completely worn out. (This is a young man's war!) A number of our men have gone to the Winchester hospital. In the past 60 hours we have had less than 2 hours' sleep. Our experience Sat. was terrible. Since Fri. we have marched 60 miles and fought 2 battles. Service under Gen. Jackson, we were told, involves hard marching and hard fighting. I think I can accept that statement now.*[168]

Riley went on to explain the challenging logistics of these Stonewall Jackson marches. The soldiers would march for fifty minutes, then rest for ten. They would repeat this formula for anywhere from fifteen to eighteen miles a day.[169]

Stonewall Jackson, from the "Great Generals" series created for Allen & Ginter's Cigarettes, 1888. *Metropolitan Museum of Art.*

The near-sixty-year-old Father Boheme thus far had managed to keep up with the regiment, but the rapidity of the marches was beginning to take its toll. Historian James Pillar claims: "For fear of being separated from the men during these rapid marches, Boheme always stayed with the encampment, refusing to accept more comfortable quarters at houses a little outside camp." Despite the pleading of the soldiers, particularly those of his Paulding parish, who did not want to send a coffin occupied by their priest back home to their loved ones, Father Boheme continued to march with the men and suffer as they did.[170]

It didn't get any easier for Boheme and the Sixteenth.

One week after the Battle of Winchester, on May 25, 1862, Kirkpatrick recorded in his diary: "Heavy rain this evening continuing nearly all night. Roads very muddy. Day's march, seventeen miles." Three days later, he wrote:

> *Aroused and…marched down to the turnpike and stopped in mud and water till day, waiting till the army passes by, then fell in and marched as infantry rear guard.…Camped soon after dark in an orchard. After getting comfortably settled, orders to fall in. Then might be heard curses loud and deep. We move a few miles and stop again for the night. Day's march over twenty miles.*[171]

Franklin L. Riley confirmed the veracity of these difficult marches in his own journal: "Marched nearly all night. Sat. it began to rain. It has rained ever since—heavy, torrential rain. To march at times we have to lock arms to steady each other or fall in the mud."[172] The marches and skirmishing and stress and fatigue and battles continued to take its toll on the young soldiers and the old…and Father Boheme.

On June 8, 1862, the Sixteenth Mississippi fought in the Battle of Cross Keys.

The men of the Sixteenth waited, hidden behind a fence. The Eighth New York Regiment marched resolutely toward them, unaware. The Yankees came within firing range, and still, the Sixteenth waited. The New Yorkers continued to march forward, confidently. The Mississippians continued to wait, tensely: two hundred yards—well within the range of a Southern rifle; one hundred yards—an easy target for a rebel young 'un; fifty yards—a squirrel stood a fair to middling chance of taking his last step. At thirty yards, the concealed Sixteenth rose and delivered a volley that decimated the stunned Yankees, who promptly fled. Colonel Carnot

Posey immediately gave the order to pursue. The Sixteenth's destination was the Federal cannon directly in their path. The Union artillery, sensing the danger, fled. Colonel Posey, sensing blood, tried to cut off the battery. He nearly did. But then, a Federal minié ball lodged in his chest. This fortuitous shot halted the advance of the Confederates and allowed the Union troops to rally. They did and nearly drove the Mississippians from the field. But the Sixteenth held their ground until reinforcements came and dispersed the Yankee counterattack.[173]

Six men of the Sixteenth Mississippi were killed, and another twenty-eight were wounded. Father Boheme went to work. There were the wounded who needed medical attention, the frightened who needed consolation and, most importantly, the mortally wounded, who needed the final sacrament before passing into the great unknown. The priest whose parish and diocese lay eight hundred miles away did all that his six-decade-old body could.

Father Boheme's final week of service and life began when the Sixteenth Regiment once again received orders to march. Once again, the destination was not revealed. The Sixteenth and their unofficial chaplain priest marched twenty-five miles from Cross Keys to Waynesboro, another twenty-five miles to the Charlottesville vicinity, twenty miles to Gordonsville, twenty-five miles to Fredericks Hall, thirteen miles to Beaver Dam Station and eighteen miles (in the rain) to a campground near Ashland, situated just eighteen miles from Richmond. There, they were told not to make any noise.[174]

The following day, the Sixteenth Mississippi Regiment ascended to the height of its fame. The Battle of Gaines Mill was a stunning Confederate victory, which forced the Union army under General George B. McClellan to abandon its plans to take Richmond in 1862. The Sixteenth lost roughly eighty men to wounds or death that day, but they were successful. They were also now immortal—at least in the annals of Mississippi military history.

Luke Ward Conerly, author of *A Historical Sketch of the Quitman Guards*, wrote:

> *About sundown, a charge was ordered all along the line, and the Sixteenth Mississippi…rushed forward to the attack, and, not withstanding the deadly fire to which they were exposed, they continued to advance….And in spite of the breastworks, the strong abates, and the galling fire, they succeeded in taking the works and driving the enemy from the field. Though this was accomplished in about fifteen minutes, the Sixteenth Mississippi Regiment lost about eighty men killed and wounded.*[175]

General Trimble confirmed Conerly's account. Trimble officially filed Report No. 255, which stated: "It is with just pride I record...that the charge of the Sixteenth Mississippi...sustained from the first movement without a falter, could not be surpassed for intrepid bravery....The Sixteenth Mississippi...numbering 1,244 men, passed under as hot a fire and [one-half mile] distance in fifteen minutes, losing in killed and wounded only eighty-five men."[176] It had been a successful and glorious day for the soldiers of the Sixteenth, excepting, of course, those eighty to eighty-five wounded, dead and dying.

One man was conspicuously not among those official casualties. In fact, he had never "officially" been part of the regiment. Father Ghislain Boheme nevertheless was, no doubt, a casualty of the campaign. While the soldiers of the Sixteenth Mississippi were sitting triumphantly around their campfires, sharing tales of their personal heroism in the day's battle, their chaplain, Father Boheme, was being placed in his coffin.

The beloved priest, utterly exhausted by the continual marches and battles and suffering from dysentery, went to nurse a sick comrade afflicted with cholera morbus. Father Boheme stayed with the suffering man all night in a farmhouse near Ashland, Virginia. In the morning, a sharp pain seized the priest's chest, and within minutes, his heart simply gave out.[177]

—•—

The End of the Sixteenth Mississippi Regiment

The Sixteenth Mississippi fought on well beyond the death of Father Boheme. In fact, the regiment was involved in nearly every major battle in the eastern theater until the end of the war. They fought at Fredericksburg, Sharpsburg, Chancellorsville, Gettysburg, the Battle of the Wilderness, Spotsylvania, Muleshoe and Weldon Railroad. They finally surrendered with Robert E. Lee at Appomattox Courthouse on April 9, 1865. By then, the regiment consisted of four officers and sixty-eight men. The Sixteenth seemed to be a magnet for battle—and they paid dearly for it.

The Sixteenth fought, and they fought frequently. But mostly, as all soldiers and armies do, they waited. They grew homesick and prayed for no more battles, no more marching, no more dead comrades and friends.

Gettysburg. *Metropolitan Museum of Art.*

J.B. Crawford wrote home to his wife shortly after the Battle of Gettysburg. His letter typifies the feelings of the men of the Sixteenth: "Tel the children I want to see them the worst in the wourld. I am mity weak, but I could wake [walk] ten miles in one hour to see them."[178] A month and a half later, he wrote again: "Martha I want to see you and the children so bad I am almost crasy. my daly prey [prayer] is that I will live to see you all once more in this life. When I think if I should never see you and the children anymore it almost make my heart bleed to think about it amen."[179]

Crawford would never see his wife and four children again. He was killed at the Battle of Spotsylvania.[180]

The seventy-two remaining men of the Sixteenth Mississippi Regiment were finally free to go home after they were paroled following their surrender at Appomattox. Ransom Jones Lightsey, of the Jasper Grays, recorded the scene, the culmination of four years of service to their defeated nation: "The soldiers were paroled as fast as possible and turned loose to get home the best way they could. We had known nothing but war for four years, but the home-journey was the tug of war. No transportation, no rations, no money, ragged and heart-sick, with miles and miles between us and our homes 'away down south in Dixie.'"[181] The ex-soldiers made their way to their various towns and cities in Mississippi.

Bishop Elder and his warrior clerics were waiting to minister to them as best they could.

July 24 to September 16, 1863

Bishop Elder spent half the day on Friday, July 24, 1863, organizing Father Guillou's belongings. Some went to the parish, some to the diocese headquarters in Natchez. That night, the bishop spent the night in his beloved friend's old room.

The following morning, Bishop Elder was up for Mass by 6:00 a.m. He spent the rest of the morning wrapping up the affairs of Father Guillou. That afternoon—perhaps, finally, with a sense of closure—the bishop heard confessions.

Perhaps to increase attendance at the confessional the next go-round, the bishop said two Masses on the ensuing Sunday morning, one at 7:00 a.m. and the other at 10:30 a.m., and he preached on the need for repentance of sins. He was back in the church at 2:00 p.m. for the recitation of the rosary and benediction. Immediately afterward, during a tremendous thunderstorm, the bishop remained behind to offer catechism class to the black parishioners of Canton.[182]

Elder spent Monday, July 27, taking care of practical matters in regard to the church and convent grounds. The highlight of the day, however, was when the bishop baptized a newborn. As he baptized the child into new life, he possibly reflected on the numbers of funerals the war had led to him presiding over and how many more funerals were likely in his immediate future. New life and death naturally go hand in hand as part of the circle of life. Yet this war was wreaking havoc on the circle, and Bishop Elder would lose far, far more of his flock than he would gain. Any baptism, therefore, would have had added significance.

The next morning, Tuesday, July 28, four weeks after the fall of Vicksburg, Bishop Elder decided it was time to finally visit the unfortunate city. He and a companion planned to travel to Yazoo City and then down to Vicksburg. The journey proved to be tedious and mighty uncomfortable. Most of the houses they passed were abandoned, and they couldn't find food for their hungry horses. When they did come across some fellow travelers, they were able to buy some corn for the horses and some cornbread, bacon and peaches for themselves. When they finally reached the town of Benton, on the outskirts of Yazoo City, they could find no room at the inn. The bishop and his companion fed their horses the last of the corn and ate their own dinner in the dark. Thereafter, they remounted and continued into Yazoo City and found lodging at the church at two in the morning.[183]

A few hours later, Elder was awake and saying Mass along with Father LeCorre. After Mass, the bishop took a quick tour of the grounds. Father LeCorre showed him the new house and lot he had just bought. A local cabinetmaker told Elder that the furniture in the house was worth a good $400. Not surprisingly, considering his recent experience on the road from Brookhaven to Canton to Yazoo City, and all the concomitant destruction he had seen firsthand, Elder suggested that the nonessential furniture be locked up for safekeeping.[184]

Elder and his friend left Yazoo City at 1:00 the next afternoon. They stopped for the night at an acquaintance's in the hopes of getting a good night's sleep before they made the difficult descent into the hell that was Vicksburg. Unfortunately, the house was so unsanitary and full of fleas that the two were forced to spend the night outside in Elder's buggy. His companion acknowledged it was the first time he had ever slept in the same room as a bishop. After that long, miserable, sleepless night, Elder doubted his friend would ever want to share a room with a bishop again.[185] The discomfiture of a sleepless night and flea bites paled in comparison with the suffering they would see in the morning.

The men awoke in the morning—or at least got up—and ate a breakfast of peaches and cornbread. They had to make a wide detour on account of the felled trees along the main thoroughfare. They took an alternate route, but it, too, was an "exceedingly rough road—hilly and badly washed."[186] Along the way, they stopped to get a drink of water at what used to be a house. Its owner gave the bishop the water and nothing else, for his house and furniture lay scattered in a pile of ashes all around him. Elder described the scene:

All his servants—40—gone. Every horse & mule taken—possibly ten pigs that might be found out of 300—Not one left of 150 head of cattle—not a vegetable nor a piece of fruit. All the clothes of the family destroyed save what they wore:—himself, wife, & children were sheltered in a very poor Negro cabin, of which the shingles were all split & curled up. They had nothing to eat but rations from the army at Snyder's Bluff—while it remained there. The poor man was telling it all apparently with cheerfulness—but at last his voice choked—& he said—"If crying would do any good, I could cry all day."—I hardly knew what to say for comfort or counsel—but I advised him to go to the camp & ask the general to give him a mule, to plough & try to raise something to eat.[187]

Fortunately, the man's family had been away when the homestead was destroyed. Still, there was nothing the bishop could say in the midst of such suffering. All he could offer was an open ear and a plea to endure.

That same afternoon, Bishop Elder visited yet another ruined home. The owner had fled north to Yazoo City but left his recently paroled brother behind. Ironically, the family was living on the largesse of the slaves who had remained on the land. The recently emancipated slaves were living off the land, selling the excess to Union troops and donating the necessities to the master's brother. The lady of the house told Elder that it had become exceedingly difficult to keep the traditional Friday fast of eating no meat. The bishop granted the family a dispensation from the customary fast. He then baptized their fourteen-week-old daughter, Eugenia. She would be the bishop's last new convert before he buried scores of other coreligionists.[188]

Elder had hoped to stay the night at the house of his newest convert but decided not to when he learned that his horse's safety could not be guaranteed. Even when one of the former slaves offered to hide his conveyance in the swamp, the bishop declined. (The bishop surely knew that the plantation's owner had been forced to borrow a horse from a former slave in order to reach Yazoo City.) Instead, Elder decided to continue on to the Yankee camp.[189]

After receiving a pass to get inside Union lines and meeting a handful of Union officers, the bishop finally found a decent bed for the evening in a Yankee tent, with his blanket directly upon the grass, and with a good mosquito net. Perhaps from gratitude, perhaps from a full stomach, perhaps from sheer exhaustion, the bishop "slept well."[190]

Finally well rested, Bishop Elder awoke in the morning, heaved himself up from the blanketed ground and rode back to report to the closest Union officer and offer his services at the Federal hospital. A lieutenant colonel from New York requested that Elder make himself available to his men by saying Mass the following morning and hearing their confessions. The bishop agreed. He spent the rest of that Saturday ministering to the sick, hearing confessions and visiting various Union commanders. It was another exhausting day. Before he retired that night, Bishop Elder walked to the top of a hill. He froze; the beauty of the moment overwhelmed him: "[B]eautiful moonlight. Something reminded me of Italy-the hills & valleys-the light-the balmy air."[191] In the midst of undreamt of destruction and suffering, the primordial, prelapsarian beauty of nature surely spoke to Elder's soul. The war would continue, the land would be scorched, many more would die (and then many more after that) and when the war was over, still more would die of its effects; a generation later, it would still not be forgotten, and one hateful action after another would create a foundation that would build a society upon oppression, revenge and violence—the cycle was doomed to repeat itself over and over, for that was the nature of man. But the hills were still there, and the valleys and the stars. And, above all, beauty. Beauty, which could never be extinguished, would endure. The land would recover. The war would end, ushering in a brief respite of peace. The souls of those he served would live forever.

True to his word, Elder prepared to say Mass for the Union soldiers on Sunday, August 2, 1863. Unfortunately, he did not have the proper accoutrements and instead elected to hear more confessions; he heard them all morning long. After lunch, he visited with more Federal officers. The bishop of Natchez, who heard tens of thousands of confessions, the seasoned psychologist, the aficionado of human nature, might have been surprised to hear the sentiments expressed in the Yankee camp, but he probably was not. The Federal officers were fighting for a cause they believed in, just like his own flock. They acknowledged that in their ranks existed numerous unsavory, un-Christian characters, just like his own nation's army. They could, and did, behave with a sense of honor and chivalry, as did many of the Confederates.[192]

Yet, inevitably, a disagreement soon erupted. A storm blew over the encampment, and the bishop and the Union representatives stayed put to discuss the intricacies of the current internecine war. Needless to say, a storm of another variety erupted. The Union officers with whom Elder was dining brought to his attention that they were the first Federal corps to enter Jackson on July 17, 1863. They immediately extinguished the fires set by the Confederate forces and stationed a guard to protect the capital city. Shortly thereafter, Jackson was turned over to another corps, and then—and only then—some regrettable happenings occurred. When Elder suggested that the extent of their army's depravities exceeded what they were willing to admit to, the conversation was terminated.[193]

With a clear decision to agree to disagree on particulars and ultimate culpability, the bishop took his leave at four o'clock in the afternoon. He rode by a plantation, spoke with the former slaves on its grounds, passed the battlefield of Chickasaw Bluff and finally reached Vicksburg four hours later. He immediately made his way to the Sisters of Mercy's convent, where he met Father Heuze. Perhaps Elder felt at least a hint of vindication when he learned that all his priest's clothes had been stolen. Just as likely, he quickly recognized that the theft of Father Heuze's clothes, which happened when the priest was away from home, was the result of a lone burglar, not the sinister and calculated machinations of a hostile enemy.

On Monday, August 3, Elder and Heuze went to visit General Ulysses S. Grant. Both clerics were stopped by the general's guard and sent to get the appropriate pass. Father Heuze, evidently aware of the bureaucratic delay created by this demand, led his bishop on a shortcut through several yards. Along the way, they stopped to pay their respects to Mr. Donovan, a parishioner who had his arm blown away by a Parrott shell while he waited next to the church door. The amputee was not home, but his young son was. The child had some malady in his eyes, and the bishop suggested he wash them out with holy water and say the Litany of Jesus each day. It seemed as if many of Vicksburg's citizens had been reduced to prayer and the hope of miracles.[194]

Finally, Father Heuze snuck his bishop to the house of General Grant. Grant's sergeant told Elder he would have to write out a request stating his purpose. Grant would then read it and decide if he would see the bishop. Elder must have been persuasive in his written communique, for the general sent word that he would see him.[195]

Elder walked into General Grant's headquarters and stood face to face with the conqueror of Vicksburg, the terror of the Confederate west. The five-foot-eight Grant looked Elder in the eye; his sharp, clever, quizzical eyes, used to command, met deep brown contemplative eyes used to persuade. Both men, quickly becoming masters of their craft—destroyer of men, ender of war versus savior of souls, buried in a lost cause—met face to face. One was destined to become the vanquisher of Robert E. Lee, liberator of the enchained and president of the United States of America. The other

Union generals holding a council of war; photograph by Timothy H. O'Sullivan. *Metropolitan Museum of Art.*

would become a resident of a defeated nation, pastor of a multiracial state and future archbishop of a Yankee diocese.

The general, known for his speed and zeal in battle, was equally prompt to grant the bishop's several requests. He told Elder that General James B. McPherson would see to the safety of the nuns' convent; he granted permission to Father Heuze to sequester a horse, buggy, forage and provisions so that he could continue his work among the Union soldiers, and he gave Elder a pass so that he and a servant could safely return to Natchez.[196]

Elder and Heuze went straight to General McPherson's quarters to get the goods and passes promised by Grant. McPherson cheerfully handed over all General Grant had promised, along with a promise that the nuns' convent would be protected and returned to them when they came back to Vicksburg.[197]

General James McPherson. *Library of Congress.*

The bishop and priest next went to Major Jared Reese Cook's house for a brief visit. The bishop had a conversation with the major's wife, Minerva, and spent some time with their two sick children.[198]

MINERVA COOK

Minerva Cook always wanted a garden. She believed that "God smiles through flowers." So, she pleaded with her husband, Jared Reese Cook, to build her a dream garden. Her husband said, "no." Then, he said, "next year." Then, "next year." Finally, all the "next years" became reality in 1858, when Minerva finally built her garden. With her husband's approval and money she had saved, she set about beautifying the family's front yard. She placed thousands of bricks to make winding walkways through the abundant and diverse flowers and foliage she put into the ground. She planted roses, spyrea, crepe myrtle, cape jasmine, evergreens, spruce, Lauramondie trees, bulbs, pinks and seeds. Under Minerva's supervision and care, her spacious plantation home was quickly becoming one of the more beautiful homes in the Vicksburg area.[199]

As her garden began to bear fruit, so did Minerva herself, for she was pregnant with her seventh child. She had experienced the pains and joys of birth six times, but this pregnancy was going to be different. This time, she would birth a girl, one she would instantly fall in love with and nickname "the seventh wonder of the world." The newest addition to the Cook household entered the world on January 27, 1859. She joined her brothers John, Samuel, Alexander, William Vincent Davenport, Charles Francis and Edward Reese. The proud parents had little Anna Malvira baptized a few months later. Life seemed enchanted for the Cook family.[200]

But it had not always been so. Minerva was not Jared Reese Cook's first wife. His first wife had died after only a year of marriage. The widowed husband was forced to deal with the grief of an untimely death early in his life. Nevertheless, the thirty-two-year-old bachelor remarried to nineteen-year-old Minerva Mary Louise Hynes on March 27, 1845. Two years later, the happy couple had their first child. Eight years later, they had their fifth, Charles Francis, or "Little Charley."[201]

Little Charley was a happy, active boy, just like his older brothers. Then, one day, just before his second birthday, he came down with a fever and chills. Only a few hours later, he was dead.[202]

Jared and Minerva were devastated. They had their little boy buried at Minerva's family plot at Asbury Cemetery. The Cooks asked that marble cover the entirety of the grave and had a hole cut into the middle, in which the coffin of Little Charley was placed. The sides and ends of the marble slab curled up in order to resemble a tiny crib for their deceased child.[203]

Life went on for the Cook family. Jared and Minerva had two more children—Edward and Anna. Their religion also helped them cope with the loss. Jared had always been a semi-devout Methodist, and Minerva was always a devoted Catholic, having been raised in the faith and enrolled at Sacred Heart Convent. As often happened in mixed marriages, the wife's religious views triumphed, and the Cook children were all raised Catholic. One of Minerva's prized possessions was her library, which contained seventeen volumes related to Catholicism. Now more than ever, Minerva leaned upon her faith. She even planned to construct a chapel in the middle of her garden.[204]

Minerva was happy with her lot in life. By 1859, she had six young, healthy children—not to mention her dream garden. The Sisters of Mercy from Vicksburg were frequent guests at her house, as was the local Vicksburg priest, who would come to visit not only her and her children but also her slaves—Minerva insisted that the Catholic slaves receive religious instruction. And, of course, these were the golden years in Mississippi—at least for wealthy planters. Cotton was king, and Jared and Minerva's slaves were its stewards.[205]

There was only one thing Minerva would change if she could: her relationship with her husband. She readily admitted that he was a good man—he was normally friendly with his children, even when roughhousing with them in the yard; he was an excellent provider; and he looked to the future (he and Minerva were sending their children to a private academy near their plantation and had agreed to send their children to Catholic boarding school when they turned fourteen). And yet, something was missing. Minerva wanted more. She wanted her husband's affection. Obviously, he spent time with her—as evidenced by the couple having seven children over fourteen years. But he also spent time in town at the billiards halls and saloons. Minerva wanted his attention and affection as well as his physical presence and business acumen. Still, she was happy and grateful to be married to such a husband, father and provider.[206]

The Cooks truly were in high cotton in 1859. Then, tragedy struck, and then it struck again and again and again…seemingly ad infinitum.

Anna Malvira had just started to crawl. The lively little baby, the "seventh wonder of the world," had begun to move. She rolled over. She crawled.

She climbed. She got into everything. She was a constant source of joy to Minerva. She would grow into a fine young girl, help her mother with little chores, blossom into a young lady, go to school, be courted by the beaus of the area, have mother-daughter talks as Minerva relived her own adolescence and youth vicariously through young Anna, walk down the aisle as her mother had done, give her mother grandchildren and comfort Minerva as she entered the winter of her life. In short, Anna was the joy, consolation and future of Minerva Cook.

Then, Anna climbed up on a cistern, fell in and drowned. She was not yet two years old.[207]

Then, Mississippi seceded from the Union on January 9, 1861. The Unionist Cooks were definitively against secession but, like most Mississippians, cast their lot with their fellow Southerners. Although they were not expecting war—at least not one that would last more than a battle or two—they had to live with the possibility of a future conflict as well as a disrupted market. Uncertainty hung in the air.

Then came the attack on Fort Sumter. Uncertainty became the certitude of armed conflict. (It would still be a brief conflict—or so everyone, South and North, believed.) The Cooks braced for such a conflict and what it would do to the marketplace.

Minerva's father died less than two weeks later.

Her oldest child, John, just fourteen years old and home for Christmas vacation after his first year at the Jesuit university of Georgetown, died from an accidental gunshot wound; the Cooks buried their third child.

Several months later, Samuel, now the oldest child, went hunting. He never came home. Like his older brother, he died tragically when he accidentally shot himself; the Cooks buried their fourth child.[208]

Then, Federal troops laid siege to Vicksburg. The Cook plantation, Hard Times, lay just behind the Union siege lines. The family was forced to watch the bombardment of their city from afar.

Then, the city that had played such a prominent role in the fortunes of their new homeland, the Confederate States of America, as well as their own lives, capitulated on July 4, 1863. The Cook family's three thousand acres were trampled, their crops taken, their fences torn and their house frequently raided. One day, Federal soldiers took the family stove. As they left, they spitefully killed the last turkey and left its carcass in the front yard. Minerva hurriedly brought it inside and fed her family.[209]

The Federal occupation of Vicksburg hit the Cook family in the same way it did the citizens of Vicksburg. Jared Reese Cook asked the local Union commander to leave behind enough food to feed his family. The officer informed Jared that he could stand in line for the proper passes like everyone else. The Cook slaves were also given a choice: remain with the Cooks and starve, be impressed into the army or go to the corrals. The majority of the slaves chose the latter.

The greatest tragedy came on April 3, 1865. Alex, William and Edward went to bed not long after it grew dark. Jared and Minerva went to bed at 9:00 p.m. This would be their last night together.

Sometime during the night, the dogs began barking. Jared arose, threw on some covering and stepped out on to the porch. He quickly ascertained that a number of soldiers in Union dress were milling about the place. One of them shouted at him to step back inside immediately. He did so, with the soldiers quickly following on his heel.[210]

The soldiers immediately set about ransacking the place—again. They found a pistol, but Jared gave them papers signed by General Grant himself granting him permission to carry the weapon. The papers also guaranteed that the Cook plantation would be subject to no more searches, and the family itself would be protected. These papers were significant, because the Cook home, Hard Times, lay in no man's land between the occupying Federal troops and the remnants of the Confederate forces—some sanctioned, some not. The two sides had agreed to respect the neutral zone. Thus, Hard Times ought to have remained in relative safety for the rest of the war. This was not to be.[211]

The Yankees took anything of value they could find, including four hams. When they asked Jared for the money he was carrying on him, he denied having any. Upon searching, they found his wallet. One of the soldiers shouted at him: "What did you tell me that lie for? I've got a notion to blow your God-damned brains out!" From that moment on, Jared feared for the lives of his family. He thought the Yankees would shoot them all and burn the house down to cover up the crime. He soon got Minerva's attention and motioned for her to go out through the front door. She did. Then she came right back to her husband with a bayonet prodding her along.[212]

Fifteen-year-old Alex panicked and fled into the woods. Nine-year-old Edward burst into the front room and grabbed onto his mother's dress. He held on tight during the interrogation.

"Where's the silver?"

"We have none; it's all been taken."

"Tell us where the silver is or die!"

"We have none."

One of the Federal soldiers then hit Minerva on the head with the butt of his gun. Another soldier stepped forward in Minerva's defense, and chaos erupted. Someone fired a shot, and Minerva collapsed to the floor. More shots were fired, and Jared was hit square in the shoulder. In a state of shock and pain, and believing his wife to be dead, Jared grabbed young Edward and escaped through a window. Thirteen-year-old William burst into the room to find his mother in a pool of blood. A Yankee soldier swung his bayonet at him, but William grabbed the barrel and held on tight. The soldier then punched him in the face. William fell to the ground, then scrambled away and hid under a bed. The soldiers, most of whom were probably as shocked as the Cooks, quickly took their leave and hurried back to their barracks. They arrived back at camp around midnight. The whole excursion to the Cooks' lasted about three hours.[213]

Around daylight, Alex returned from his hiding spot in the woods. William crawled out from beneath the bed. The brothers cautiously walked to the front of the house and found their mother lying in blood but alive. Bewildered and frightened, Alex asked his mother: "Why did they shoot you?" A dying Minerva could only gasp: "They shot me for no reason."[214]

A concerned neighbor alerted the authorities, and Minerva was moved to her bed, where she spent her final hours. She said little but requested that her children be raised Catholic. As to her murderers, all she could say was that they were black men wearing Federal uniforms. Sometime between two and three o'clock in the afternoon, Minerva went to join her daughter, her sons and her father. She was buried in Asbury Cemetery.

The *Vicksburg Herald* summarized the robbery gone bad:

> On the night of April 3rd, after Major J.R. Cook, who lives seven miles from Vicksburg, and his family had retired, a party of about 25 negroes entered the house and shot Mrs. Cook. Major Cook sprang to her assistance and was severely if not mortally wounded. Supposing his wife already dead, he succeeded in making his escape in company of his little son. The negroes remained in the house five hours, plundering. Mrs. Cook died the following morning. She spoke but few words, merely saying she had been shot by negroes dressed in uniform. Major General Dana has offered a reward of $500 for the apprehension.[215]

The Federal soldiers were, in fact, apprehended (and eventually prosecuted), but that was little consolation to Jared Cook and his remaining children.

Henry Johnson was the carriage driver for the Cook family. He was born a slave and was destined to always be a slave—until Ulysses Grant and the Union army captured and liberated Vicksburg. Like many of his fellow former slaves, Johnson flocked to the Federal lines. He enlisted in the army and was given a blue uniform and a rifle.[216]

One night, he and a number of his fellow freedmen soldiers were talking and decided they would hunt some rebels. The Cook plantation became the agreed-upon destination. Johnson made no objections. He knew the Cooks well. Minerva had always been a demanding taskmaster. Some considered her fair, but she was a difficult woman for whom to be a slave. Minerva was a hard worker, and she had no qualms about doing the necessary household chores herself. She even rewarded those slaves who imitated her work ethic. Once, she gave a wedding for two of her favorite hardworking slaves, Lou and Robert. She gave them a lavish dinner and hired a band to play at the afterparty. That party went on all night in the slave quarters. Yet, as Johnson well understood, it was still a slave wedding. Lou and Robert would soon be back to the day-to-day slave's lot of making a profit for others.[217]

Johnson did the work required of him, but he was not one of Minerva's favorites. If laziness was near the top of Minerva's list of vices, then thievery was at the summit. If Minerva had slaves whipped for idleness, then Henry Johnson never wanted to experience the punishment for stealing. However, he almost did.[218]

One day, Sister Mary de Sales, the superior of the Sisters of Mercy, visited the Cook plantation. Minerva often had local clergy at her home to visit her children as well as those slaves who wished for instruction or sacraments. In the meantime, she developed a happy and lasting friendship with a number of the sisters. On this particular day, Henry Johnson saw an opportunity to steal the Mother Superior's shoes. He was caught in the act. However, the gentle nun somehow kept him from receiving a lashing—or worse. Johnson never forgot the black-clad white woman who saved him from punishment.[219]

Just a few years later, Henry Johnson sat in a prison cell awaiting execution. He and twelve others had been charged with conspiracy to commit murder, robbery, attempted murder and murder. Between May 2 and May 6, 1865, the thirteen men sat in the Vicksburg courthouse before a military tribunal. After hearing testimony, the judge sentenced nine of the charged men to death by hanging. The punishment would be carried out in three weeks just outside the city limits.

Historic Warren County courthouse, Vicksburg, Mississippi. *Ken Lund*.

Sister Mary de Sales, upon learning the fate of these murderers, was filled with compassion and pity. She began visiting the jail cell each day and ministering to the condemned. It did not take long for Henry Johnson to confess his guilt and ask for forgiveness. In that dank prison cell, the Catholic Church received its newest member when Henry Johnson was baptized.[220]

On the day of execution, May 26, 1865, Johnson and the eight other convicted men rode to the gallows with their hands behind their backs, sitting on the coffins they would soon occupy. As they passed the house of the Sisters of Mercy, Johnson looked up and saw Sister Mary de Sales standing on the balcony holding a crucifix containing the body of the condemned and executed Jesus. Johnson respectfully lowered his head.[221]

When asked for his final words, Johnson exclaimed that he only wished that Christ's blood would wash away his sins. His face was then covered, and the support beneath him was kicked away. Henry Johnson rocked, suspended in the air, neck broken, until he went and stood before the Christ he had called upon.[222]

On August 4, 1863, twenty months before the untimely death of Minerva, Bishop Elder celebrated Mass in the morning in the Cooks' parlor. The family, aided by the Sisters of Mercy, who stored their belongings and sometimes stayed at the Cooks' home, had established an altar in the parlor when Vicksburg first began to be bombarded months earlier. Throughout the siege, the altar never moved. When the Federal troops finally took Vicksburg, they ransacked the house, and the nuns' goods were stolen, damaged or strewn about the house.[223]

After Mass, Bishop Elder was visited by General Grant's surgeon, Dr. Hewitt, the same man who pleaded with Union officers to not burn St. Peter's church in Jackson. Hewitt brought with him a Catholic woman who had fallen away from the faith and now wished to return to Elder's flock. The bishop spent a fair amount of time speaking with her. He then had a much deeper and personal conversation with his host, Jared Reese Cook, than he was able to the night before. Elder noticed that Cook "is a good deal depressed with the state of things but still bears all patiently."[224] As glum and depressing as Cook's life was now, it would not begin to compare with the tragedy he and his family would soon endure.[225]

After his depressing meeting with Cook, Elder walked through the streets of Vicksburg. What he saw was painful. He had expected to see emaciated and downtrodden Mississippians who had just endured forty-seven days of a dehumanizing siege; indeed, he did see that. But he also witnessed the suffering and neglect of countless recently freed black people. He blamed the Federal bureaucracy for their predicament. Clearly frustrated, that evening, Elder ranted in his diary:

> The negroes are dying in the streets of Vicksburg. The Federal Army expresses a willingness to feed all of them - but there is such a multiplicity of offices in the town that some of the Negroes can hardly find out who to apply to. But those who had plenty are exposed to sickness from change of place, & diet - & water & from want of some one to look after them. No exercise - no occupation - separated from old associations - naturally wanting in energy- no cleanliness- no foresight - no comforts - no medicines - Dr. Hewit [sic] says they suffer from homesickness, depression of spirits - & just give themselves up to sink.[226]

The destitution of the former slaves saddened the bishop, and he began to make inquiries on their behalf. He received no satisfactory answers. As far as Elder could surmise, the Federal government had no policy toward the former slaves of Vicksburg—or the South, for that matter. The Union officers seemed to believe their mission was to free the slaves, thereby depriving the Confederacy of their servitude. Beyond that, there seemed to be no clearly defined policy. As Elder claimed, "as far as the Fed. Govt. & Army prevail, the race will die out like that of the Indians."[227]

After inquiring as to the future of the emancipated slaves, Elder returned to town to find his buggy had been accidentally broken by a recklessly driven Union wagon. Nevertheless, Elder himself had to pay for the repairs—in Federal dollars. He then tried to buy a hat to protect himself from the scorching August sun but learned he needed a permit to buy anything. He demurred and instead went home to eat and sleep at a parishioner's house.[228]

The following morning, Wednesday, August 5, Elder arose and made his way to the Sisters of Mercy convent. The previous days had prepared the bishop for disappointment, and that is exactly what he found. Two of the porch columns were knocked down; a shell had passed through the house, damaging a number of walls; and Union general Elias Dennis had allowed his servants to carry off the nuns' "plates, dishes, tables &c." and other valuable belongings.[229]

Elder then made his way over to the church, where he found more destruction, though not as severe as at the convent. Nevertheless, the bishop counted nine holes in the building, including a large one made by a Parrott shell in May 1862—the same day that Mr. Donovan lost his arm while standing at the church's front door. It was fortunate that there were no more casualties during that bombardment. Father Bannon had been in the sacristy preparing to say Mass when the shell burst into the window above his head and exploded over one of the altars. Another shell tore the leg off the chair on which a "soldier was sitting talking to Father Heuze tearing his coattail to ribbons."[230]

The parishioners told Elder that they believed the church had been targeted. Will Tunnard, a soldier from Louisiana stationed in Vicksburg, agreed. Tunnard wrote in his journal that the Yankees had seen people congregating near the church, and they "instantly opened on them with a Parrott gun. As the shells came screaming wickedly through the streets, exploding or entering the building, men, women and children hastily sought shelter to escape the danger....Such unheard of, ruthless and barbarous methods of warfare as training a battery of rifled canon upon an assembly of unarmed men and worshipping women is unparalleled in the annals of history."[231]

William Henry Elder, bishop of Natchez. *Archives of the Diocese of Jackson.*

The following morning, Bishop Elder traveled to the Louisiana side of the river. He found a camp full of ex-slaves, many of them simply waiting, seemingly with nothing to do. He met one man lying sick along the shore. When the bishop inquired, the man claimed to have worked for three straight weeks on behalf of the Federal government but couldn't find out who was responsible for his pay. Consequently, he now sat destitute along the banks of the Mississippi River. Elder gave him enough money for breakfast and went on his way.[232]

That same afternoon, Bishop Elder arrived in Grand Gulf, thirty miles south of Vicksburg. The sight of the former prosperous and bustling town stunned the bishop, who had thought he had become acclimated to the inevitable suffering caused by war. The buildings and houses simply were not there anymore—"scarcely any chimneys standing."[233]

With a heavy and aching heart, Bishop Elder finally concluded his depressing trip through Yankee-occupied central Mississippi. The odyssey had taken thirty-one days. In that one month, the bishop had seen destruction and death on a scale he had never before witnessed. He saw firsthand the displacement of hundreds, perhaps thousands, of individuals, many of whom he had personally known in happier days. He saw the destruction in two major cities, and he witnessed the shattering of the social order that had existed not only in his beloved and adopted Deep South but also in the Maryland where he had grown up. For worse and for better, Bishop Elder was now part of a "world turned upside down."[234]

Yet, on another front, Bishop Elder's world had not changed at all. In his worldview, he was part of an institution that transcended the times. Although his churches might be bombarded, even destroyed, his Catholic Church remained intact and immortal. Although Bishop Elder was certainly an avid reader of the various *Times*, he was also a student of the eternities,[235] and he understood that his church and mankind would endure.

The morning after Bishop Elder returned to Natchez, he paid a visit to the Sisters to take stock of events in Natchez over the month he was gone. The next day, he visited the orphans at D'Evereux Hall. On Sunday, August 9, 1863, the bishop said Mass, visited with a couple of callers, then agreed to a dispensation granting his parishioners the ability to eat meat on Fridays and feast days. (For many who lived in the war-ravaged regions of Elder's diocese, meat had become more difficult to obtain. There was also no refrigeration, so when meat became available on a Friday, the people needed a dispensation to eat it then.)[236]

The following day, Bishop Elder paid a call to General Thomas E.G. Ransom, who was in charge of the Natchez occupation. The twenty-nine-year-old general struck Elder as young and "girlish in his looks." Despite his effeminate appearance, Ransom was a hardened veteran. He had already been wounded in four battles, including Fort Donelson and Shiloh. General Ransom had an unusual visitor that day—the son of J.F.H. Claiborne, the Confederate owner of Laurelwood Plantation on the coast and Dunbar Plantation in Natchez, who had been feeding sensitive military information to the Federals as well as money in the form of a tax so that he could continue with his illicit trade. Obviously, Elder was unaware of the arrangement of the elder Claiborne and exchanged pleasantries with the son.[237]

Five days later, Elder received another interesting visitor. Dr. Hewitt—the man who had tried in vain to prevent the destruction of St. Peter's in Jackson and had helped carry out the church's valuables before it was engulfed in flames—arrived to pay his respects to Bishop Elder. He had ridden to Natchez with his boss, General Ulysses S. Grant, and stayed for dinner. Previously, Elder and Hewitt had discussed opening an orphanage in Vicksburg for black children. This initial discussion had taken place at Jared Reese and Minerva Cook's plantation, Hard Times, in Vicksburg. Now, Dr. Hewitt was again pressing the matter. He told Elder that former slaves were dying by the score of scurvy and various diseases. Consequently, more and more children were being left without parents. Dr. Hewitt had taken it upon himself to send a letter north to the fathers of the Holy Cross requesting their aid. He wanted to make sure that Elder would accept such help. The bishop told the good doctor that he would in no way object. He did, however, ask Dr. Hewitt to make sure the orphanage was operated and funded by "people of the North" and connected to the Federal army. The bishop was concerned that with the war still going on and, as of yet, undecided, he not be ensnared in a legal imbroglio, for no one was certain of the status of those in the Federal camps. If the South won, the black orphans were slaves; if the North won, they were free; but if a truce—or ceasefire—ended the war, who would responsible for feeding and taking care of the orphans? No one knew. Elder did not want to accept charges for whom he could not provide.[238]

The next day, Sunday, August 16, Father Finucane delivered the homily at St. Mary's. He spoke of the love of God, and the collection went to the orphans of Natchez. The collection plate was full of both Confederate and Federal money—although, by this point, Confederate money was greatly depreciated and not accepted in most establishments in Natchez. After dinner, Elder sent Father Finucane to the black camp, known as the corral, to check on the condition of the former slaves who had recently fled to Union-controlled Natchez. Finucane reported on the deplorable conditions of the camp and told the bishop that he had baptized thirty infants in just a few hours.[239]

The following day, Bishop Elder accompanied Father Finucane on a visit to the camp. As they neared the camp, they passed a number of black men "marching under white officers." Elder assumed the men were part of a work detail. When Elder and Finucane got to the gate, they found it guarded by black sentinels. Inside the corral, they saw thousands of people and countless rough, low-ceilinged cabins made of boards with plank roofs and windows made by leaving a plank sticking out of one side of the structure. Glancing around, Elder noticed there were few healthy men about the place. Most had already been marched out of the camp to participate in drills or work for the Federal army. Instead, the place was filled with women, children and the feeble, sick and dying. The bishop was told that "of those that sicken seriously – very few get well."[240]

Elder walked about the camp in shock. There were so many sick, suffering and dying. The Federals seemed to have provided the camp with plenty of bread and meat but had neglected to provide fruit and vegetables. As a result, many of the former slaves were dying of diarrhea and dysentery. With no medicine and little attention, the recently freed slaves were dying by the dozen. Elder baptized twenty-four babies that afternoon, twenty-three of whom were at the point of death.[241]

The bishop also met a few Catholics among the camp's residents, who were referred to as "contraband,"[242] including Frank Evans of Calvary, Kentucky. Evans was a twenty-two-year-old former slave who, in Kentucky, had been a devout Catholic and regularly received the sacraments. Now, in the Deep South, he lamented to Elder, he was not allowed to go to Mass or confession. Elder promised Evans that he would now be welcomed at the bishop's own house whenever he desired to confess.[243] Elder left the camp that afternoon with a heavy heart.

The next day, the bishop was immediately busy with his priestly duties. With Father Finucane back at the camp, Elder took Communion to a housebound parishioner, then visited the orphanage at D'Evereux Hall. His mobility was hampered when his horse, Gentle, became sick that afternoon.

To make matters worse, Father Finucane returned home complaining of pain in his back and limbs.

Father Finucane was feeling better by morning, but things only became more depressing for Elder. His esteemed horse, Gentle, died at midnight. Then, he visited the orphanage and was once again reminded of the devastation of the war—not only on the battlefields, but at home. He next visited a sick parishioner, as if he needed another reminder of the frailty of life. As he made his way home for a brief respite, a heavy storm descended on Natchez. The sky seemed to weep for the misery of the land. It also was a portent of darker days to come. As if to prove the latter, a parishioner came to tell Elder that another of his flock, Martin Culhane, had been killed six weeks ago at Gettysburg. With a heart growing heavier by the minute, Bishop Elder raised himself from his evening meal and went to visit Culhane's mother.[244]

Thursday, August 19, 1863, was another dreary, rainy day—hardly the palliative for a burdened spirit. In addition, Father Finucane fell sick again but was able to eat dinner with his bishop and the visiting Colonel Alexander Chambers. However, the following afternoon, the exhausted priest began frequently vomiting, and a sore on his leg began to look worse. Bishop Elder sat with him for much of Saturday. At some point during the day, the bishop requested that the Federals begin to do a better job taking care of the orphans. Perhaps frustrated, perhaps in a moment of clarity, Elder recorded the cause of the orphans' suffering that night in his diary: "It is the presence of the Federal Army wh. causes their present destitution, by making the money of the community unavailable, & depriving the people of servants, teams & other means of furnishing provisions."[245]

Putting his frustrations aside, at least for a couple of hours, Bishop Elder immersed himself in Mass the following morning. The liturgy for the day required Elder to speak of one of the numerous lepers of the Gospel. He must have had Father Finucane's own deteriorating physical condition in mind as he delivered a homily comparing the healing of the leper to the healing of the deformity that is sin by the sacrament of confession.[246]

Elder spent the following week visiting the Federal hospital and found a number of Catholics, especially from Kansas. Father Mathurin Grignon visited more Federal troops and former slaves on the other side of the river. That Friday, August 28, the skies opened up on Natchez. It rained so much and so hard that the basement of Elder's presbytery filled with six inches of water. But, as floods do, the water eventually receded. If only the flood of sick and orphans and widowed and wounded arriving each day seeking the ministrations of Elder and his overworked priests would begin to recede. However, the war in the Diocese of Mississippi was doomed to continue for nearly two more years.[247]

The following week was more of the same, with Elder visiting the sick, administering last rites and visiting the black camp to give what solace he could, particularly when it came to giving the sacraments to black Catholics. It was during one of these frequent visits that Elder first stumbled upon the black hospital—previously, he had not recognized it as a hospital.

As soon as the bishop opened the door, he saw a dead man, with his hands tied, on the floor. The stunned bishop then saw a young boy lying in the middle of the floor on some rags, dressed only in a shirt, "apparently dying," breathing hard as he desperately fought for air. The bishop knelt beside the boy and offered what comfort he could. The boy was still conscious and seemed to desire what Elder had to offer; the bishop promptly baptized the boy and gave him absolution. As he rose, the bishop heard an aged man calling Elder to "Come & pray for him." Elder obeyed and walked over to a ninety-two-year-old man lying in the corner. The moribund man eagerly accepted Elder's instructions and agreed to follow the Catholic Church and its teachings and to live those teachings should he ever recover. The next day, Bishop Elder gave his newest convert the last rites and a scapular[248] to assist him on his heavenly journey. The man accepted both with "sensible devotion."[249]

Elder was back in the black camp the following day, this time with Dr. Brady, a Federal Catholic. Brady pointed out a number of the irrecoverable sick, and Elder spent the afternoon with them, instructing, exhorting, anointing and baptizing. That day, he baptized sixteen new parishioners, mostly infants.[250]

On Sunday, September 6, Father Picherit rode into town to help his bishop by saying Mass at St. Mary Cathedral. Elder noted in his diary that afternoon that Father Picherit had collected more than $1,000 in Confederate notes. Either the parishioners were unloading their tithe via increasingly useless currency, or many still held out hope that the Confederacy's fortunes would soon be revived.[251]

Father Picherit returned to his parish at Brookhaven on Monday. Father Finucane left the following day to head to his new post at St. Michael in Paulding, Mississippi. Bishop Elder attempted to relieve his anxiety at having lost valuable help by yet again visiting the black camp and baptizing ten more souls.[252]

A young Father Henry Picherit. *Archives of the Diocese of Jackson.*

On Wednesday, September 9, Elder must have taken satisfaction in announcing that the Natchez Catholic schools would be reopening the following Monday. Father Grignon would oversee the schools, with Mr. Corbett acting as principal.[253]

The joy of overseeing schools, with the concomitant witnessing of the young growing and flourishing and seeing the students with starry eyes and bright futures, was counteracted by visits to the black camp over the next several days to administer to those "prepared…for death."[254] But these were part of his flock as well.

That Sunday, Bishop Elder preached his homily on "the greatness of the Priesthood."[255] Having served as a priest for a decade himself, Elder no doubt appreciated the role of those who, at the grassroots level, battled the world, the flesh and the devil. Now, as bishop of Natchez, he was still, of course, a priest and pastor at heart. Yet he was also the administrative head of the diocese. Few bishops in the country were under such constant duress.

The Natchez Catholic schools reopened on Monday, September 14, 1863. Elder noted: "Very small attendance."[256] Perhaps the depreciated Confederate

A young Father Mathurin Grignon. *Archives of the Diocese of Jackson.*

currency was to blame, or the uncertainty of the future that made parents rethink the cost of a Catholic education or the number of potential enrollees who were now orphaned and called D'Evereux Hall home.

Wednesday, September 16, 1863, proved to be an eventful day for Bishop Elder. After paying a visit to a parishioner, the bishop ran into a former classmate from Mount St. Mary's. Federal colonel Bernard Gaines Farrar, of the Thirtieth Missouri Regiment, paid his respects to his old acquaintance. At that time, Farrar was trying to raise a regiment of black soldiers. Throughout the war so far, slaves in the Confederate states were freed by Union troops in an effort to deprive their masters of military and agricultural labor. Then, they were enlisted in Federal camps to serve as cooks, ditch-diggers and officers' servants. Now, they were being hired as soldiers. (Three months earlier, their black brethren at Milliken's Bend had offered their opinions on the dependability and value of black soldiers. Black soldiers—most of whom were recently recruited freedmen—fought a small but important battle to defend Grant's supply depot fifteen miles northwest of Vicksburg. Confederate troops hoped to cut off Grant's supply line but were driven off by the black troops despite the fact that the latter were inexperienced and

Seated black soldier wearing frock coat, gloves and kepi. *Library of Congress.*

had inferior weapons. The battle made many white people on both sides rethink the capabilities of black soldiers. General Grant himself praised the valor and efficacy of the black soldiers.)

In the meantime, Elder continued to visit the black camp. He saw the destitution and despair. Granted, Elder often visited the camp during the day, when the strongest and most able residents were already out on work detail. He saw the most impoverished, the sickest, those closest to death. Elder had spent most of his time in the corral's hospital and knew how inadequate it was. He relayed this information to Colonel Farrar in hopes that it might be improved. The colonel promised to bring the state of the black hospital to the attention of his commanding officer, General Walter Q. Gresham.[257]

That same afternoon, as well as the following morning, Elder was back at the hospital, the improvement of which he had been campaigning for so ardently. In those thirty-six hours, he baptized twenty-nine people. However, this time, he met with some opposition. Most of the former slaves in the corral were Protestant, Baptist, in particular, and not too well disposed toward Catholicism. Some of Elder's other priests, and certainly the nuns working in his diocese, faced similar indisposition.

The Hospitals

Throughout the war, Bishop Elder had too few priests to minister to his soldier-parishioners abroad and those on the home front. He was often in a position in which he had to allocate the priests to one group at the expense of another. The bishop made his decisions based on the principle of triage: those who stood in the presence of death would receive priority care. Thus, throughout the conflict, whenever a battle appeared imminent, as it did in early April 1862 in the vicinity of Corinth, Elder would order all priests in the area to leave their parishes and position themselves around the army. Inevitably, death was the offspring of battle. Elder wanted all who faced such a reality to have access to the sacraments—particularly confession and the Eucharist. As a result, many a Catholic soldier went to his death with the consolation of a final unburdening of his soul and a firm belief that his sins had been forgiven.

For every soldier who died on the battlefield, two more died in the hospitals. While Bishop Elder prioritized priestly service on the battlefield, he placed nearly as much emphasis on their presence in the numerous military (and civilian) hospitals hastily constructed across the state. His reasoning was simple: people were dying in the hospitals. They were suffering, scared and in need of the consolation that only religion could provide. Of course, the bishop wanted his clergy and nuns to focus on the Catholic invalids, but he also asked that they treat their Protestant brethren. After all, a Protestant was a potential convert—and even if he was not interested in converting, he was still a human, a creation of God,

Union field hospital in Savage Station, Virginia, after the battle of June 27, 1862. *Library of Congress.*

deserving of respect and dignity as he suffered (and many eventually died) in the overcrowded hospitals.

Because of Elder's policy of prioritizing hospital work, many of his priests and many more of his sisters spent a significant amount of time ministering to the sick, wounded and dying in the myriad hospitals across his diocese.

One account in particular emphasizes the horror of the Confederate hospitals in Mississippi and the heroism of those who tried to bring some solace to those forced to endure their own private hell in the infirmaries.

Kate Cumming was a native of Scotland and resident of Mobile, Alabama. When the Civil War erupted, her mother and two sisters returned to England. Kate, however, elected to remain behind with her father and brother. A Confederate and humanitarian, she served as a nurse from 1862 to 1865 and was active in Mississippi, Alabama and Georgia. Her diary offers a detailed, intimate and cathartic look inside Mississippi's Civil War hospitals.

The first impromptu military hospitals in Mississippi were built in April 1862 in and around Corinth, the site of the first major battle in Mississippi. When word reached Kate Cumming in Mobile that a massive battle, the largest the continent had seen, was imminent in either southern Tennessee or north Mississippi, she and a number of other concerned women, nurses and surgeons headed in that direction.

Cumming was on a train headed toward Corinth on April 7, even as the Battle of Shiloh still raged. She was eager to play her part in the war and frantic over the fate of her brother, who had enlisted in one of the many Confederate units engaged in the epic battle. Only able to get as far as Okolona, sixty miles from Corinth, Cumming wrote in her diary the night after she left Mobile: "I can see nothing before me but my slaughtered brother, and the bleeding and mangled forms of his dying comrades." The wind, the storm and the "raining in torrents" did little to lift her spirits as she anxiously awaited news from the front.[258]

The following morning, April 9, Cumming was allowed to visit some of the train cars that had arrived in Okolona from the battlefield. She noted that "a number of ladies have come from Natchez, Miss., to join us." The sight of the wounded in the train was but a foreshadowing of what she would find two days later, when she was finally granted permission to enter Corinth. At least, these wounded men were healthy enough to travel south by rail.[259]

When Cumming and her companions arrived in Corinth on April 11, it was still raining. There was water and mud everywhere. The women in her party dispersed to different hospitals, with Cumming going to the one established in the Tishomingo Hotel. Others had tried to prepare her for what she was about to see. "But alas! nothing that I had ever heard or read had given me the faintest idea of the horrors witnessed here. I do not think that words are in our vocabulary expressive enough to present to the mind the realities of that sad scene. Certainly none of the glories of the war were presented here."

Confederate and Federal soldiers were lying side by side, crammed wherever a parcel of floor showed. The mud had made the roads too bad to move the men, and the sheer number of wounded and dying led to inevitable overcrowding. There weren't enough medics to treat them. There wasn't enough food feed them. A typical dinner consisted of bread and butter and tea or coffee—the latter without milk. Their plight, and the plight of those charged with treating them, would only grow worse over the next week.[260]

Kate Cumming spent her first twenty-four hours like she would spend her next six weeks. Though utterly exhausted after staying up all night bathing wounds, she found the time to record that first evening in her diary: "The men are lying all over the house, on their blankets, just as they were brought from the battlefield. They are in the hall, on the gallery, and crowded into very small rooms. The foul air from this mass of human beings at first made me giddy and sick, but I soon got over it. We have to walk, and when we give the men anything kneel, in the blood and water." That night, she sat and prayed with a sixty-year-old man who lived near Corinth. Just before the battle, he went to visit his two sons serving in the Confederate army. Seeing his boys, and knowing it might be for the last time, his fatherly instincts kicked in, and he shouldered his own musket, intent on sharing whatever fate awaited them. Now, he sat in the hotel-turned-hospital with only one leg.[261]

Cumming coped with the shock of her new vocation by commiserating with, leaning on and lifting her fellow volunteers. A number of these women came from Natchez. Cumming was impressed with their gentility, devotion and kindheartedness. She wrote of one such Natchez resident the first night she arrived at the hospital: "[The woman from Natchez] has been

Womans Mission by C. Schussele, engraved by A.B. Walter. *Library of Congress.*

constantly by a young man, badly wounded, ever since she came here, the doctors say that she has been the means of saving his life." In the weeks to come, Cumming would become close friends with a number of the Natchez residents from Bishop Elder's diocese.[262]

Two days after arriving in Corinth, Kate Cumming saw her brother. He was haggard and exhausted but alive and unwounded. Certainly, this reunion lifted her spirits, as she spent the next several days treating and ministering to those soldiers who were not so lucky. Some lost limbs, some lost their minds and some died. All of them suffered.

Before the first week was over, Cumming met Mrs. Glassburn, another Natchez volunteer, and the two became close friends over the next month. She also met and worked with the Sisters of Charity. She noted that the doctors seemed to prefer the sisters as nurses not only for their experience but for their quiet endurance.[263]

April 17, 1862, five days after her arrival at the hotel hospital, was a trying day for Cumming. It began with her doing her usual morning task of cleaning and feeding the wounded. She was "washing the faces of the men, and got half through with one before I found out that he was dead. He was lying on the gallery by himself, and had died with no one near him." There seemed to be a silver lining that afternoon, when one of her patients, a Mr. Wasson, with whom she had grown particularly close, seemed to be progressing, and both he and Cumming thought he would soon be discharged and on his way home. But then, the doctor told Cumming that Mr. Wasson would not survive the day. She was devastated. When she went back to her new and soon-to-be-departed friend, she could not hide her anguish, try as she might. Wasson noticed and asked why she was so upset, but Kate could not bring herself to tell him the truth. Instead, she asked if he was afraid to die, to which Wasson replied no, he wasn't, but being so young, he would like to live some more and see more of life. In particular, he wanted to see his mother and father once more. Kate later wrote in her diary: "I did what I could to prepare him for the great change which was soon to come over him, but I could not muster the courage to tell him that he was going to die."[264]

Finally, the doctor himself came to Wasson and told him what Kate could not: he was going to die that very night. Wasson instantly turned pale and silent. After a while, he turned to Kate and said: "Sister, I want to meet you in heaven." He then begged that he be allowed to see his two brothers, who were also wounded and in Corinth hospitals. Unfortunately, his two brothers couldn't be located before Wasson died.[265]

Wasson did, however, survive the day and into the early morning hours of April 18. At four o'clock in the morning, he looked over and noticed that Cumming, who had been sitting with him the entire time, looked utterly exhausted. He asked her, then begged her, to get some sleep. Finally, she acquiesced and went to bed. When she came back later that morning, she saw that Wasson was dead. One of his companions had taken her place and said that he had died peacefully—a small solace to the woman who had become so attached to the man and who, just twelve hours earlier, was so happy that he would soon be heading home.[266]

The same day Mr. Wasson died, Dr. Foster of Natchez arrived to bring some of the wounded home. Enough of them left that Cumming and her new friend, Mrs. Glassburn, moved over to College Hospital. Cumming was pleased to find that "the Sisters of Charity have charge of the domestic part, and, as usual with them, everything is parfait. We were received very kindly by them." Kate Cumming and company immediately and enthusiastically went about their customary duties.[267]

Cumming quickly realized that an alarming number of soldiers were dying each day at her new post. Those who were destined to recover had almost certainly done so already by the end of the first week of her arrival. Those who did not recover faced an uphill battle that would last weeks, months or possibly end in a coffin—as long as the Confederate government in and around Corinth could keep up with the demand for wooden coffins. It seemed as if Cumming's services had been transferred from a hospital to a hospice.

On April 22, in the middle of Cumming's second week of service, a good number of patients were moved out of College Hospital in anticipation of another great clash. The rumors of another encounter must have sent shivers through not only the soldiers who would be forced to fight the follow-up to the deadliest battle in U.S. history but the medical staff who would be forced to deal with the aftermath. While the soldiers would fight a one- or two-day battle, the medical corps would fight to save the wounded and dying-but-not-yet-dead over the foreseeable months.

The following morning, with the storm clouds of battle still hovering above the hospital, Kate Cumming arose and tried to comfort a young man who was to have his arm amputated that day. The child, turned into a man before his time, accepted his fate—not the fate of a lost arm but of death, for no one in that hospital had yet survived the amputation of a limb. His prognostication of doom was soon fulfilled.[268] Cumming saw the sun the next morning; the amputee did not. However, he lived in her memory when she passed by the hospital on an errand. She glanced in the direction of where the young man had died; she beheld an arm she did not recognize. Later that night, she recorded the sight in her diary: "A stream of blood ran from the table into a tub in which was the arm. It had been taken off at the socket, and the hand was hanging over the edge of the tub, a lifeless thing."[269]

Cumming completed her errand and returned to her duty at the hospital. It didn't get any easier for her that day. She recorded: "There is a Mr. Pinkerton from Georgia shot through the head. A curtain is drawn across a corner where he is lying to hide the hideous spectacle, as his brains are oozing out."[270]

The weather the next day aligned with Cumming's mood—rainy and gloomy. The day brightened when another Natchez woman showed up at the hospital. Mrs. Noland proved to be a "very devoted nurse" who treated all the soldiers as if they were her own sons. She explained her motherly devotion to Cumming: her own son was fighting in the Confederate armies to the east. She felt certain that if he were wounded, some other kind nurse would treat him the same way she was treating her patients. This philosophy sustained Mrs. Noland during the dark hours of the trying hospital work.[271]

The day after Mrs. Noland's arrival, Kate noted: "Three men have just had their limbs amputated. This is so common that it is scarcely noticed." Just as soldiers who had been fighting long enough became desensitized to the violence around them, so, too, did the medics become accustomed to the horrors of the aftermath of that violence.[272]

The days became monotonous as Cumming got used to the constant sickness, moaning, agony and death. Tuesday, April 30, offered a brief respite from the horrors of hospital duty. Mrs. Glassburn received some gifts from Natchez. Among the gifts were many wines and delicacies, as well as some much needed furniture. Mrs. Glassburn, Kate Cumming and the other nurses took great delight in distributing these gifts to their patients.

The joy of their "Christmas in April" was short-lived, for two days after they received the generous package from Natchez, they could hear cannon fire on the outskirts of town. At seven o'clock that evening, the wounded began trickling into the hospital.

The wounded continued to come into the hospital by ones and twos and threes—a steady stream. Cumming and all the other medics feared the stream would become a flood when the follow-up battle occurred. All were aware that the Federal army was advancing upon Corinth, and all were apprehensive about the consequences.

Cumming spent Sunday, May 4, reading and talking to the wounded soldiers. One patient in particular caught her attention. He was a thirteen-year-old Texas boy who had lost his leg in a skirmish. His father, a cavalry man in the same unit, the Texas Rangers, stayed with his son throughout his ordeal. Cumming noticed that he was exceedingly proud of his boy.[273]

The young Texas boy made a deep impact on Kate, as did the lack of chaplains serving the hospital. She wrote: "We have no chaplain to attend the sick and dying men; they often ask for one. I have thought much of this, and wonder why chaplains are not appointed for the hospitals….We profess to be a Christian people, and should see that all the benefits of Christianity are administered to our dying soldiers."[274]

The need for on-site chaplains was obvious when an eighteen-year-old boy died after having his leg amputated. Not only were there no chaplains present, there wasn't even a coffin in which to bury the young soldier; Federal troops had recently destroyed the factory that made the coffins.

More and more wounded continued to come to the hospital over the next few days. Some had served the Confederacy, some the Union. Those who died were simply wrapped in a sheet and placed in the ground.

The stream of wounded soldiers was beginning to surge. Throughout the next week, the incapacitated arrived hour by hour as the skirmishing became more intense. The weather was growing oppressively hot, and the hospital staff began to succumb to stress and exhaustion. One day, Cumming heard particularly heavy firing on the outskirts of town. With the advance of the Federal army and the increasingly unsanitary conditions, the majority of Cumming's patients were evacuated. Then, the surgeons were called to the front in anticipation of the climactic battle that would decide the fate of Mississippi—and possibly the Confederacy.

The battle never came. Nevertheless, Cumming went south, back to Okolona, while her Natchez friend, Mrs. Glassburn, went by train even farther out of harm's way to the hospital in Brookhaven.

Even though Kate Cumming was now in Okolona, the wounded continued to arrive at her new hospital. She wrote in her diary on May 31, 1862: "While at the train this afternoon, I saw a number of men taken off the cars and laid on the platform; some were dead, and others sick or badly wounded. They were wrapped in their blankets, and put down as if they were bundles of dirty rags. No one seemed to notice them. O, how my heart sickened as I looked at the sight!" Unfortunately, the wounded continued to arrive. Over the next three years, the trickle that became a stream became a river and, finally, a flood of biblical proportions.[275]

Cumming's duties continued into June. Her most memorable patient was not a soldier at all but a sick child—the war was beginning to wreak havoc on citizens as well as soldiers. Ministering to this sick child nearly broke Cumming's heart. She recorded the tragedy in her diary: "I sat up all night with a very sick child….The poor little thing suffers a great deal; the mute appeals for aid, which you have no power to extend, are truly touching; and I think I felt as bad, if not worse, at the sight of this sick child's sufferings, as I ever did at the sight of any of the sick or wounded whom I saw at Corinth."[276]

One week later, Kate Cumming left the war in Mississippi for the war that would soon begin in Alabama. Her odyssey had just begun. So had that of countless other Mississippians.

September 17 to October 25, 1863

Bishop Elder spent mid-September 1863 trying to get compensation for damaged church property in Natchez, particularly a fence and some hay that had been taken by "Colored People" and Union soldiers for housing and campfires. It was a long, bureaucratic process. However, despite the fact that Father Orlandi had been unsuccessful in receiving compensation for the property damaged in Jackson under his watch, Bishop Elder was far more effective. He received promises that the church fence would be fixed and that the convents in both Natchez and Vicksburg would be respected.[277]

Elder then turned his attention to the black camp, where conditions were still unsanitary and deadly. He went directly to General Walter Q. Gresham about the humanitarian crisis at the corral. Gresham promised to do what he could. In the meantime, General Gresham gave passes—good for all roads and all hours of the day—to Elder, Father Grignon and the recently ordained Father O'Connor. The clerics immediately availed themselves of the generous passes by visiting the corral as well as the hospital of the black regiment at Forks of the Road. Incidentally, this regiment, comprised of recently freed black Mississippians, was bivouacked where one of the nation's largest slave markets had been. Unfortunately, the conditions at the military hospital and the barracks were not much better than in the corral.[278]

Having found this human misery (and potential converts), Bishop Elder began to spend more time with the black troops. In fact, he spent the first half of October moving back and forth between the corral, barracks and military hospital. Elder did not neglect his duties to his white parishioners. He continued to say Mass on Sundays, met with the trustees of D'Evereux Hall to raise money for the orphanage and visited the sick of his flock, including a young girl named Beatrice who was dying of diphtheria. She died the following day, as did a number of people in the corral and barracks.[279]

On Friday, October 16, 1863, Bishop Elder began a devotion of forty hours. He, his priests and his congregation would kneel before the Blessed Sacrament, in turns, for forty straight hours. Elder offered up the sacrifice for peace and an end to the war. Pope Pius IX had requested such an observance beginning on this day and had voiced his request through Elder's superior in New Orleans, Archbishop Odin. For Bishop Elder and the majority of Mississippians, the end of the war could not come fast enough.[280]

On Saturday, after his shift at the forty-hour devotion, Bishop Elder performed a duty commensurate with his role as judge.

Mary Friery was wedded to Michael Maher. However, she did not wish to be. She pleaded with Bishop Elder to annul the marriage so that she could get out of it and be free to contract what she called a true marriage one day. Mary did intend to find a husband; she just didn't want it to be Michael Maher. Unfortunately for her, the two had already been married by a justice of the peace. Now, Mary, who, along with Michael, was a practicing Catholic, claimed that she only went through with the ceremony because she was pressured by her father. She swore to Elder that she had never wanted the marriage. Furthermore, both parties insisted that the marriage had never been consummated. Elder was quite sure that the marriage was not valid due to lack of sincere intent and no consummation, but he asked for more time to consider the case. Both sets of parents agreed. Before he left, the bishop hinted to Michael Maher that he should let Mary go.[281]

The same afternoon that Elder investigated the Maher-Friery marriage, he learned that an "outrage" had been committed on one of the "children of the Asylum" (orphans). Elder immediately reported the violation to the Federal authority. He followed up on the case the next day, Sunday, October 18. The guilty party showed up at Elder's house to explain himself, but the bishop, disbelieving the offender's explanations, asked him to leave and informed him that his case was now in the hands of the provost marshal. Ironically, Bishop Elder preached that Sunday on "Reparation." Perhaps he had in mind the inexcusable "outrage" committed against the little orphan girl. Afterward, Elder received a visit from Union general Alexander Chambers.[282]

The week of October 19, 1863, saw Elder performing his now usual chores about Natchez—pleading for compensation on behalf of destroyed and damaged church property (now, it was the cemetery fence), visiting the corral ("number much diminished - sickness also"), administering to the black troops at the Forks of the Road, paying respects to various Union generals (Crocker and Gresham) and doing his best to see that the most vulnerable of his flock were protected. Elder was especially concerned with the plight of his impoverished congregants. When the war began, a number of them had come to him and turned over what little income they had for safekeeping. The bishop had agreed to hold their money in trust. Now he was worried that he would be forced to turn it all over and thereby further impoverish the already destitute of Natchez. He brought his concerns to General Gresham and asked his advice. That night, Bishop Elder recorded the conversation in his diary:

> *I explained to him how all the deposites came into my hands - as a favor to poor men & their families. He told me not to be uneasy. - He did not think anything wd. be done to molest me in the case. I explained our general position : viz. that we did nothing to bring about the war. When it was begun, we like many in the North wished our own side to win, especially when we saw what evils the South wd. suffer from being subdued. But we had never preached war sermons - nor urged people to go to war. Our desire was to do good to souls - we labored for all souls in our reach, from North or South. Personally I was willing to bear true allegiance to any govt. Russian or Kamschatkan - but I did not wish to do anything wh. wd. injure my usefulness among my flock.* [283]

This diary entry by Bishop Elder is a wonderful summation of the role of the Catholic Church during the Civil War. Of course, each Catholic bishop, Southern and Northern, had unique views of the war, but the institutional church's position was, as it always had been, to save souls. And everyone—Northerners, Southerners, white, black, rich, poor, Catholic and Protestant—possessed a soul worth saving.

—•—

THE CORRAL

Tens of thousands of jubilant slaves flocked to the Federal lines surrounding Vicksburg during the summer of 1862. They were seeking something they had never experienced: freedom.

Within weeks, more than one thousand of them were sent, in the summer heat of 1862, into the swamps and bayous surrounding Vicksburg with the Herculean task of rerouting the Mississippi River. Their new white commanders immediately set them to what General William Tecumseh Sherman called "a pure waste of human labor"—not to mention lives.[284]

The former slaves began working on the bold plan to divert the Mississippi River under the orders of General Benjamin Butler, who delegated the task to his subordinate, General Thomas Williams. Within four weeks, the project was abandoned. Dabney M. Scales, of the Confederate navy, wrote an account of the experiment while aboard the CSS *Arkansas*:

> *Some of our men went over the river to where the Yanks were working at their canal—Williams Ditch, as they call it. They found about 600 Yankee graves, but worst of all they found about 500 Negroes, most of them sick, and all left in the woods without anything to eat—or any provision whatever being made for them. They say they were worked hard in mud and water where their soldiers refused to work—And when they were taken sick, they were turned off to hunt a home, probably many miles distant—They were shot down like dogs, because they left the trench when we threw shells among them. This is the way the Yankees treat the race for whose freedom they pretend to fight.[285]*

The plan was revived six months later, when General Ulysses S. Grant ordered the completion of the canal. The project changed from Williams Ditch to Grant's canal, but the results were the same. A disgusted General Sherman wrote to his friend and commander: "The river is about full and threatens to drown us out. The ground is wet, almost water, and it is impossible for wagons to haul stores from river to camp, or even for horses to wallow through." Again, the project was called off—this time for good.[286]

But it was too late for one of Elder's clerics, Father Basilio Elia. Father Elia had been working amongst the Union troops mired in the swamp and suffering from fever and dysentery. Many of the Yankee soldiers were Catholic and were dying by the hundreds with no priest to administer last rites. Elder

Vicksburg Canal by Adalbert John Volck. *Metropolitan Museum of Art.*

gave Elia permission to cross lines to do what he could to help. Father Elia did much—until he caught dysentery. He died on April 3, 1863.[287]

Still, the former slaves continued to flood into Vicksburg when they heard news of the Federal victory. All rejoiced at the freedom that had been denied to them for so long. What some of them found was poverty, sickness, delusion and death.

The sheer flood of black people pouring across Union lines became an issue for every Federal army in the Deep South. After January 1, 1863, the former slaves became freedmen. In many cases, they went to work for the Federal army. However, Union commanders were flummoxed as to how they were expected to provide for these new charges. The quartermasters had prepared to feed companies, battalions, regiments, brigades, even entire corps, but few seemed to know how to clothe, feed and shelter these new freedmen. When General Sherman returned to Vicksburg from his triumphant march from Meridian, he noted a line, ten miles long, of black people trailing his army. The majority of these freedmen descended upon Vicksburg.[288]

The Union answer was to place them in camps, often called corrals. Quaker missionary Henry Rountree visited a number of these camps and was aghast at what he found. During an early visit, he saw people huddled in cowsheds and wrote, "poor wretchedly helpless negroes, one man who had lost one eye entirely, and the sight of the other fast going.…They had no bedding, two old quilts, and a soldier's old worn out blanket comprised the whole for 35 human beings."[289]

For those Federal officials who genuinely tried to help the freedmen, it seemed as if they had taken on a Sisyphean task. There were 4,500 civilians living in Vicksburg after its capitulation. The Federal occupiers could call on the services of 7,500 soldiers, but there were now 25,000 former slaves living in the overcrowded city.[290]

The corral in Natchez was hardly better. Natchez resident and diarist Annie Harper recorded her impressions of the camp:

> *The most pitiable of all was the condition in which the negroes from the country were plunged, in their haste to "go to freedom." On every road they came in crowds, mothers carrying their babes, with every size and age streaming along behind. The day of jubilee had come—nearly all left, food, clothing, & fires behind in their forsaken homes. They were gathered near the cities by the thousands in what were called "Kraals" without food or shelter. The Gov't issued rations to this great army of the unemployed, and for a short time they realized the bliss of freedom, to be fed and to do nothing—the negro wants no better heaven, but when the soft summer skies had gone and winter blasts set in, they succumbed to cold and the most terrible diseases the result of filth, and their unrestrained appetites. Along the river bank at Natchez, eleven thousand lie buried to whom freedom brought indeed a rest from their labors—The same was true of every post in the South, especially on the river bank the mortality was awful. The odors from the Kraal were disgustingly perceptible at the distance of half a mile. A servant of Mrs. Anna Darden's having lost four children there, returned home to her mistress, preparing to risk as she supposed the chance of Slavery again, to remaining. Many sent word to their old master "for God's sake to come and take them home."…The Catholic Bishops reported at Head-quarters that it was not a fit abode for wild beasts.[291]*

Annie Harper's racial views aside,[292] her journal makes it clear that at least some of the newly freed black people did not find themselves in an enviable position; nor would many former slaves or their descendants for another one hundred years—or longer.

On Saturday, October 24, 1863, Bishop Elder again visited the corral. The weather was "very cold." The freedmen inside the encampment clearly needed attention, and soon—winter was coming.[293]

The following day, Elder delivered a homily on the motherhood of Mary and stressed her value as a model to all parents. The bishop may have again reflected on the importance of his own mother and father. He may have thought of the orphans down the street who no longer had mothers or fathers on account of the war. He may have meditated on his own role as metaphysical father of a war-stricken diocese. Had he done enough? Was he a worthy vicar of Christ? Perhaps the overworked bishop was haunted by the words in Matthew: "Whatever you did for one of the least of these brothers and sisters of mine, you did for me."[294] Still, he continued to labor on behalf of the least—and the rich, the entitled and the abandoned.

After this, Bishop Elder disappeared for two months—or, at least, his diary entries did. Of course, Elder continued to perform his apostolic duties. His successor four times removed, Bishop Richard Oliver Gerow, who did so much to preserve the memory of his predecessor and the history of the Natchez-Jackson Diocese, wrote: "Between October 25 and December 22, 1863, we find no entries. Were these pages lost, or were the intervening dates never written in Diary form? I do not know."[295]

December 22, 1863, to June 25, 1864

On Tuesday, December 22, 1863, Bishop Elder made the following diary entry: "Reached home after 8 weeks absence." He immediately got back to work.

Elder preached two Masses on Christmas Day—one at 4:00 a.m. and the other at 10:00 a.m. One week later, on New Year's Day, 1864, the bishop again preached the 10:00 a.m. Mass. He then traveled to a new hospital that had opened during his hiatus: the smallpox hospital. Located at Mrs. Ogden's country estate, the hospital was almost entirely filled with former slaves. Just as he did at the corral, barracks and military hospital in town, Bishop Elder got to work ministering to those some considered the least of his brothers and sisters.[296]

A few days later, Elder found the state of his white orphanage, D'Evereux Hall, "untenable" as he visited the children. The fence that he had been campaigning to have fixed was now entirely gone. That evening, he met with the trustees to determine the fate of the orphanage.[297]

The following morning, a distraught Father Orlandi arrived from Jackson and presented to Elder his plan to approach and receive compensation from General Ulysses S. Grant for the wanton destruction of Catholic property in Jackson.[298] The bishop gave his approval but likely doubted the efficacy of such a request.

The next four days were filled with meetings about the fate of D'Evereux Hall. The condition of the building had deteriorated to the point that both Bishop Elder and the trustees determined to move the orphanage. A committee was appointed to seek a new location.[299]

When the bishop traveled to D'Evereux Hall to make the overseer priest, Father Miller, aware of the board's decision regarding the orphanage, he learned that nearly all of the priest's ducks had been stolen the night before. It seemed as if Elder and the board's decision had been immediately justified.[300]

On Friday, January 22, 1864, Basil Thomas, a black man from Louisiana, showed up at Elder's door. Thirteen months earlier, the bishop had been visited by the Kane family, white neighbors of Thomas, who told Elder of a black Catholic man who lived near them and had been severely beaten on a number of occasions for refusing to work on Sundays. In December 1862, Bishop Elder, moved by the man's perseverance, had sent him a rosary. Now, the man was at his doorstep. Elder invited him in and gave the eager and pious Catholic the sacraments. The two spoke for a while, and Elder was impressed enough with the devout Basil Thomas to record the scene in his diary that night and note the exact date when he had first heard of the man's story.[301]

As heartening as Thomas's visit was, Elder was immersed in the tragedies of a fallen world just two days later. One of the orphans at D'Evereux Hall, Josephine Dixon, was suffering terribly from smallpox. Elder paid her a visit that Sunday. The following day, Josephine's classmates and fellow orphans began a retreat at the sisters' place. Josephine was not with them. She was breathing her final breaths nearby in the smallpox hospital. In the morning, she was dead. Elder had hurried over just in time to give her one final blessing before she entered eternity.[302]

Things did not get easier for Elder as the last week of January 1864 drew to a close. On Saturday, January 30, Father Finucane arrived from Paulding. Elder's youngest priest had been ordained after the war had started and was in perpetually frail health, but he had already done his share of ministering in various cities, battlefields and hospitals.[303] After supper, the bishop and priest had a lengthy visit. It is clear that Elder had grave concerns about the efficacy of his young priest, for the following Saturday, he advised Father Finucane to leave the diocese and enter a religious order. Father Finucane promptly rejected that suggestion, and Elder countered by giving him a letter of introduction to Reverend Lavialle of St. Mary's College in Kentucky. He also gave his struggling priest a personal letter. He granted Finucane a three-month sabbatical and urged him to seek a position in another diocese.[304]

That same morning, Elder buried one of his parishioners, John May. He also lost another good horse, Dixie. After he posted a ten-dollar reward, the horse was returned to him the next day; Father Finucane and John May were not, nor were the hundreds of sheep he had lost over the last three years.[305]

On Friday, April 8, 1864, Elder traveled north toward Vicksburg. He arrived the following morning at seven o'clock and said Mass. He did the same the next morning, Sunday, February 10, and preached a homily concerning the Good Shepherd. With so many of his flock, both white and black, endangered, the bishop may have questioned his own skills as a shepherd.[306]

The shepherd tried to visit more of his flock in Yazoo City the next morning but was unable to get there and resolved to stay in Vicksburg for another week.[307]

That Tuesday, he wrote a letter to President Abraham Lincoln that concerned a controversy that would be dissected, revisited and debated for more than a century. It involved an issue that went back to the times of Constantine, Giles of Rome, John of Paris and St. Thomas More. Where exactly is the line between church and state drawn for a bishop and his secular counterpart?[308]

Bishop Elder had been instructed, as had all Mississippi clergy in Union-occupied cities, to offer a prayer during their Sunday services for President Lincoln.

Elder was in a difficult position. The war was not over. He was living in what he believed to be a legitimate, though occupied, state. His duty as a citizen, therefore, was ambiguous. If the rebellion was lawful, then the occupation might prove temporary; Confederate forces might rally and drive out the Federals. In that case, offering a prayer for the leader of a foreign occupying army would put the bishop in an awkward position with his fellow Southerners when they returned.

In addition, even if the Federal occupation proved permanent, Elder was still the shepherd of his Southern flock. Submitting to the highly unpopular Federal request would make it more difficult to lead his flock if his sheep viewed him as a traitor.

Finally, Elder had no intention of being told by secularists and Protestants how the Catholic Mass was to be conducted.

Just before Elder left Vicksburg for the return trip to Natchez, he made a visit to Union general John McArthur and asked that the convent of the Sisters of Mercy be respected. After filling out the necessary paperwork, the general promised that the sisters could retake possession of their convent when they returned to Vicksburg.[309]

As he returned to Natchez, Elder began to question a decision he had made in Vicksburg, and it pained his conscience during the seventy-mile return trip. Distraught by the constant bloodshed and the continuous wanton destruction of property, Father Francis Orlandi had begged Elder's permission to return home to his native Italy. Although he was loath to part with such a devoted and necessary pastor, Elder finally relented during his Vicksburg sojourn, and the loyal but psychologically damaged Father Orlandi returned to the land of his birth.[310]

Elder arrived in Natchez at two o'clock in the morning on Thursday, April 21, 1864. Thirteen hours later, he was on his way to Port Gibson to visit a sick friend. It took him a full day to get there, as the roads were in disarray. He also saw a good number of carriages broken down alongside the road—there simply weren't enough able-bodied people to fix either the roads or damaged conveyances.[311]

Having finally arrived in Port Gibson, Elder decided to spend the weekend in the sleepy, conquered, stunned town. He wanted to offer the Catholics there a chance to partake of the sacraments of confession and the Eucharist. He was hurt that so few took advantage of the graces he was offering.[312]

Less than a week later, the bishop was on the road again. He wrote: "Horseback traveling so far agrees well with me." This was a good thing, too, for Elder would spend much of the next year in the saddle.[313]

The bishop rode through the town of Rocky Springs and was soon stopped and questioned by some scouts. Fortunately, one of the officers recognized the bishop from his service to the wounded and sick in the Port Gibson hospital, and Elder was allowed to continue his journey.

The following day, the bishop rode through Raymond and must have thought of the terrible carnage there the previous year, when a Confederate brigade accidentally engaged an entire Federal division. Thoughts of Father Francis Leray, who was present at the battle and reportedly galloped across the battlefield to tend to the fallen and the dying, must have filled the bishop with pride and gratitude.[314]

If, in fact, thoughts of his warrior-priest lifted the spirits of Elder, they were soon deflated upon his reaching Jackson. The capital city's church, St. Peter's, had been restored yet again—this time, it was above an engine house several blocks away from its original site. The new church was "fitted up very tasteful and comfortably," and Elder found no complaints with the building or the congregation. Rather, he was frustrated with himself for having allowed the able Father Orlandi to depart the diocese for Italy. The Catholics of Jackson were hungry for a pastor. Three different heads of families, including the wealthy and influential Hubert Spengler, offered their houses as a rectory for a priest. They promised to pay and provide for one should Elder decide to give them another. The bishop went to bed that night with a heavy conscience. "My uneasiness at allowing Father Orlandi to go away is unhappily confirmed."[315]

Elder stayed in Jackson, now also known as Chimneyville, for ten days, during which time he performed the customary ministries of a local pastor—the pastor he himself had removed from the people of Jackson. He spent hours in the confessional, confirmed the newest members of his flock and said Mass.[316] He also sent a letter to the Sisters of Mercy who were working at the hospital in Shelby Springs, Alabama, and asked them to return to their convent in Vicksburg as soon as feasible. If the sisters felt they could not leave the hospital in good conscience, he asked that at least some of them return to occupied Vicksburg. Elder was determined that some sort of normalcy be returned to his suffering flock in west Mississippi.[317]

On May 7, 1864, Elder left Jackson for Canton. Along the way, he visited a patient at the insane asylum, which, oddly, had been hit by a cannonball and a number of bullets during the siege of Jackson when Federal troops established a front just outside the building.[318] He arrived in Canton that same day and visited with Father Huber. Both bishop and priest stayed with Franklin Smith. Smith had lost his slaves and horses in the last Union raid but had gained a wife as coreligionist. His wife was intent on receiving the sacrament of confirmation and joining her husband's church. She and the bishop spent the evening conversing about various aspects of Catholicism. According to Elder, "she took a deep interest in all my explanations."[319]

The following morning, Elder celebrated Mass before a scant audience. Disappointment with the attendance at Mass soon compounded when he learned that Father Huber had authorized Franklin Smith to sell the church's frame kitchen for $400 in Confederate notes. Elder saw the rapid depreciation of Confederate currency in Natchez and was not only pastor of the entire state of Mississippi but also the chief administrative officer, so, perhaps understanding the economics of the time better than most, the bishop was not pleased with this sale. He believed that Father Hubert and Smith had sold the property for far less than it was worth. But upon interviewing the parishioners, Elder decided to let it go. After all, the kitchen was aging and in danger of catching fire and burning down the church building. Coincidentally (or perhaps not), Father Huber left that afternoon for St. Mary of the Immaculate Conception church in Sulphur Springs.[320]

This church also proved to be a challenge for Bishop Elder's diocesan vision. A fair number of slaves working the surrounding plantations were Catholic. Their bishop did not want to deny them the opportunity to practice their faith. Furthermore, Elder strongly believed that a good Catholic must know his faith. Therefore, Elder had previously demanded that the parishioners of St. Mary of the Immaculate Conception build a thirty-foot addition to their church so that the black Catholics of the area could attend Mass. He had also tasked the now-deceased Father Guillou to instruct the slaves in catechism. A handful of white women helped Father Guillou by teaching the female slaves the basics of the Catholic faith. Because few slaves were attending these catechetical courses, for various reasons, Elder had asked Guillou to ride to the surrounding plantations owned by Catholics and visit the slaves.[321] By the time Elder arrived in Sulphur Springs, Father Guillou had been dead for a year, and many of the black Catholics he had served were in the corrals of Vicksburg and Natchez.

At the same time that Bishop Elder was trying to ensure that slaves would have equal access to the sacraments and Mass, a large proportion of his white parishioners in Sulphur Springs were enlisting in the Confederate army to ensure that these same black Catholics would remain enslaved. Most of those white parishioners would find themselves in the ranks of the Eighteenth Mississippi Regiment. This doomed regiment would see much action in the Virginia theater, and they were with General Robert E. Lee when he surrendered at Appomattox. By that time, only four officers and forty-four men remained.[322]

On May 10 or 11, Elder went to visit Dr. Michael O'Reilly, a wealthy Madison County slaveholder who now found himself the master of a lonely plantation, his slaves having fled to the safety of Union lines. The bishop's Mississippi odyssey nearly ended on this May afternoon. He and his horse were riding over a small bridge when the bridge broke. Rider and horse plunged eight feet into the water beneath them. Fortunately, neither were hurt, although the horse's girth and bridle were broken. Elder realized how lucky he had been. His propensity to travel alone could have made the fall far more serious, potentially even deadly. Nevertheless, he continued on his journey to Canton. That evening, he arrived at Dr. O'Reilly's house only to find the doctor in a depressed state of mind. O'Reilly sent the bishop to stay with a neighbor that night. However, Elder was back at O'Reilly's in the morning and found his friend in better spirits; Elder said Mass and offered up the service in gratitude for his narrow escape the day before.[323]

While Elder was visiting with another Canton parishioner, Oliver Luckett, he learned that the Federal troops were rapidly advancing on Canton. Luckett immediately gathered his slaves, livestock and whatever he could easily carry and hurried away. Bishop Elder agreed to stay behind and watch his children. The bishop had done more than his share of preaching, teaching, forgiving sins, saying Mass, ministering to the sick and wounded and preparing souls for death since the war began. Now, he could add babysitting to his list of wartime duties.[324]

Fortunately for the citizens of Canton, the notice about the advance of the Federal troops had been a false alarm; the troops were not even on the eastern side of the Big Black River yet. Oliver Luckett returned home and relieved his bishop of his temporary charges. Elder said Mass at the Lucketts', took lunch with another parishioner and headed east toward Sulphur Springs.[325]

Elder was reunited with Father Huber in Sulphur Springs. Luckily for Father Huber, Oliver Luckett had vouched for his sale of Sacred Heart church's kitchen in Canton. Elder's concerns about the sale must have been somewhat alleviated; that afternoon, he appointed Father Huber as pastor in Jackson. He insisted, however, that Father Huber visit the parishes in Sulphur Springs and Canton once a month. Elder then returned to Canton with a pass from Confederate general Wirt Adams that would get him to Yazoo City.[326]

After a couple of days in Canton, Elder headed northwest to Yazoo City. He said Mass at 8:30 a.m., then toured the town. Earlier that week, Union troops had burned more than a dozen houses and the courthouse. The Catholic church itself had lost one of its posts and suffered a broken stove when a Yankee cannonball had penetrated the building two months earlier. It was also pockmarked by a number of minié balls.[327]

Elder remained for a week in Yazoo City, where he made the plantation of Mrs. Wilkinson his headquarters. He spent his time mostly with those in the black community who had not fled to Federal lines. He instructed them in the faith, distributed first Communion and confirmed those who determined to permanently enter the church. The night before he left, Elder reflected on his time in war-torn Yazoo City: "Mrs. Wilkinson has been much blessed. She has not been at all disturbed on the plantation. Her house in town was burned. All her servants remain with her. The family too appear very happy together." Elder spent one last happy breakfast at the mansion of Mrs. Wilkinson, then made his way back to Canton.[328]

Upon his arrival at Canton, Elder learned that General Wirt Adams had given the necessary passes to the Sisters of Mercy who had been working in the Shelby Springs, Alabama hospital to return to their convent in Vicksburg. The bishop immediately made his way to Jackson. When he arrived, he was told that Father Francis Xavier Leray and four of the sisters had departed that morning for Vicksburg under a flag of truce.[329]

Elder spent the night of Sunday, May 29, 1864, in Jackson. The next morning, he set out for Port Gibson but stopped for the night in Raymond, the site of the battle that had sealed the fates of Jackson and Vicksburg one year earlier. In the morning, Elder was on the road again, but first, he baptized the children of an Irish Catholic family in Raymond and urged them to attend confession in Vicksburg at their earliest convenience.[330]

Forty-three miles later, Bishop Elder reached Bayou Pierre, just ten miles from Port Gibson. However, his horse refused to wade through the water. The bishop had no choice but to plunge into the darkening waters and lead his transportation to the other side. Wet, and then cold, Elder finally reached his friend Mr. Moore's house at ten o'clock that night.[331]

As was his habit, Elder rose early in the morning and said Mass at the Moores' home. He then set off for Port Gibson, arrived, spent the night, awoke early and said Mass. He then visited a dying parishioner and gave her last rites.[332]

The following morning, Elder journeyed to Rodney, twenty miles southwest of Port Gibson. He spent the entire day baptizing people and hearing confessions. The following morning, he heard more confessions, said Mass and was on the road by ten in the morning. One of his grateful parishioners traveled with him and helped him to cross over Cole's Creek, and Elder was on his way. When he was only a few miles from Natchez, the bishop realized that he would not make it into the city before curfew. So, he decided to spend the night in Washington, which was fewer than seven miles outside his see. There, he stayed with Mrs. Hazlip and "learned positively that no one is allowed to come out of Natchez without taking the Oath of Allegiance to the United States." The bishop knew that a bitter confrontation was awaiting him at his destination.[333]

In the morning, Elder said Mass at Mrs. Hazlip's. Afterward, the mother of two soldier-boys approached him and begged for news of her two sons. These were the conversations that weighed heavily on the bishop, for he had to tell the anxious mother that her boys had both been wounded. After teaching catechism to some of the slaves, Elder rode to the Perrault house, about five miles away, and spent the night with the worried family. In the morning, he said Mass and performed a few baptisms; that evening, he wrote in his diary: "The family all well, but anxious about their boys."[334]

After visiting the Perraults, the bishop was only fifteen miles from Natchez, but he was determined to visit another parishioner outside the city. Elder realized that his future actions in Natchez might deprive him of the chance of visiting his flock on the outside of the city. Therefore, he was determined to see as many as he could while he could.[335]

Unfortunately, and surprisingly, since he was so close to home, Elder got lost and spent much of Monday, June 6, 1864, riding around the outskirts of Natchez. Along the way, he was mistaken for a Federal soldier by Confederate scouts. Luckily, they held their fire, and once they properly identified the well-known and respected cleric, they led him to the road he was looking for. After riding to the homes of different Catholics and letting them know that he planned to say Mass in the morning at the Norton house, he headed to the Nortons'. He got there at 8:30 p.m. One would expect the bishop to be irritable and exhausted after having lost a day wandering about, mostly lost. Instead, he seemed to be in a devious—if not a jovial—mood. Elder approached the house and attempted to frighten the family by acting the part of a Federal soldier and demanding that they reveal the whereabouts of the rebels. He later wrote: "[I] did it so well, that I got frightened myself." In the end, the bishop revealed his true identity, and the family undoubtedly went from shock and terror to relief and jubilation that it was only their bishop, and that he was going to stay the night with them.[336]

Elder found the Norton crew—Mrs. Norton, Sophy, Maggie, Agnes Haggerty and Felix— in good spirits after his practical joke. In the morning, they were joined by four other women of the area, and Elder said Mass at seven o'clock. Afterward, the bishop decided it would be prudent to remain outside the Union lines until he could hear something more definitive about the happenings in Natchez.[337]

After a visit with Confederate captain Wilmer Shields, Elder decided to travel south to Woodville. The move would accomplish three things: he would be forty miles farther away from the authorities in Natchez, he would get to spend some time with his brother John and he would minister to the Catholics in the area. Therefore, he planned to spend a few days in Woodville, say Mass for that community on June 12 and return to Mrs. Norton's for the June 19 Mass. Captain Shields swapped horses with Elder for the journey. (Elder's horse, Dixie, had sore spots on his back and hind leg on account of the bishop's recent relentless traveling.)[338]

Three days later, Elder was on his way to Woodville. When it began to rain, he pulled over and sought shelter with a hospitable family. When the showers ceased, he rode on to the ferry only to find that the swamp was currently impassable. He returned and spent the night at the home he had left just hours earlier. Elder tried again in the morning to reach Woodville but was again frustrated when he learned from passing Confederate soldiers that the alternate route was also impassable. Surprisingly, two of the Confederate soldiers who spoke with Elder recognized him from his time in Maryland, for they, too, had been students at Mount St. Mary. The bishop and students-cum-soldiers exchanged pleasantries before Elder returned to the Norton residence outside Natchez.[339]

Elder had decided to reverse his schedule and spend a week with the Nortons, then travel to Woodville. He put his new itinerary into action by saying Mass at the Norton house on June 12, 1864. Mrs. Perrault arrived the next day with her son Thomas. More visitors came to pay their respects to Elder throughout the week. In fact, it was a very pleasant respite for the bishop, who had endured so much hardship and suffering over the previous two years. At the end of the relaxing sojourn, Elder wrote in his diary: "I wrote letters—wrote up a part of my acc. books.—read a little Theology. It was a very pleasant week, only it passed away too fast. A commodious room—spacious gallery & grounds—every convenience & attention to make me comfortable. Mass every morning. Night prayers."[340]

On the morning of Sunday, June 19, Bishop Elder again said Mass at the Nortons'. He was well pleased with the attendance and noted that night in his diary the names of a number of that week's congregants. Not surprisingly, they were almost all women—the men were either fighting or dead.[341]

After Mass, Mr. Perrault rode up to escort his wife home. The previous Tuesday, she had been stopped by Yankee cavalry who questioned her extensively about the area, and she was still rattled by the experience. In fact, two Union cavalry did appear at the Nortons' that day. They were searching for black men in order to impress them into service. Elder was relieved that the only black man on the place was out trying to track down some hogs. Had he been around, the bishop feared that the soldiers would've taken the man and mounted him on the horse he himself had just borrowed from a friend, Captain Shields.[342]

In the morning, Elder again tried to get to Woodville. Fortunately, this time, when he arrived at the ferry, he ran into some Confederate soldiers who had recruited a local black man to guide them through the swamps; Elder joined the group. The journey over the next ten miles was a harrowing experience for the bishop. Negotiating their way through the domain of alligators and cottonmouths was unpleasant in and of itself, but at least they were mounted—until the brackish water, too dark for any man to see what lurked beneath, became too deep even for the horses. The men were forced to dismount and walk across fallen logs, carrying the saddles and baggage while the horses swam across. Finally, the nightmare ended, and Elder exited the swamp fourteen miles above Woodville.[343]

When he reached his destination, Elder was pleased and then stressed to find his cousin Edward and his family in a state of panic, as word had just reached them that Federal soldiers were presently making their way toward Woodville. Remembering the fate of Jackson and Yazoo City, Elder must have been alarmed by the news. Fortunately, it was a false alarm, and the Elder family passed the night worried but safe.[344]

When the family awoke, their houses and livestock untouched, the bishop said one of his more unusual Masses, for it was celebrated in the home of a Jew. The owner had gone away and offered it to the Catholics of the area free of rent. One of the rooms was turned into a chapel, and Elder noted that it was "a very pretty" place to celebrate Mass.[345]

Later that day, Elder traveled north toward Clinton to get a pass that would allow him to cross the river and visit Baton Rouge. The Confederates had recently made an attempt to crack down on illicit trade with the enemy, hence the need for a pass. Irritated at being forced to double back from a direction in which he had just come, Elder nevertheless complied. He vented some of his frustration that night in his diary when he wrote: "Reached Clinton at night. Lazy people—dirty table—dirtier room. No sleep for mosquitos." To make matters worse, the owner of the house in which Elder planned to stay was asleep when he arrived, and the bishop was forced to sleep elsewhere.[346]

When he awoke in the morning, Elder paid his respects to Mrs. Elder, whose husband, Edward, was his cousin. There, he learned of the misadventures of several of his family members. Elder's daughter Eleanor and Bishop Elder's niece Celeste (his brother John's daughter) had set out for Bay St. Louis with one of their cousins the previous week. When they got to the Tangipahoa River, Celeste nearly drowned. Fortunately, she survived, but the buggy carrying the three broke down. Because of the war and its consequent depopulation of many areas of the state, they could find no one to fix it. Then, they learned the roads leading to Bay St. Louis grew gradually worse, and they would have great difficulty finding food and lodging along the way. The three decided to return to Clinton. From Clinton, they made their way to John Elder's place in the country near Baton Rouge. Bishop Elder had just missed the trio.[347]

Elder got the necessary pass and then made his way back toward Baton Rouge. One of the Confederate pickets he passed complained about the futility of their jobs: the pickets stayed at their posts day and night to keep

A young William
Henry Elder.
*Archives of the
Diocese of Jackson.*

people out of Baton Rouge, but every day, people poured across the river as if through a sieve. It seemed getting a pass was as easy as asking for one. Elder seems to have held his tongue and not commented on the bureaucratic quagmire he had been wading in over the last couple of years. Instead, he passed by the disgruntled sentinels, pulled over when it began to rain, ate a dinner of blackberries and arrived at his brother John's around five o'clock that evening.[348]

Elder was happy to see not only John but also the three cousins who had departed a half-day before him. They had safely arrived a few hours ahead of him. The bishop was saddened to learn exactly how difficult the war had been on John. His brother had been arrested and imprisoned despite there being no charges against him. Eventually, he was released, but his house and land had been plundered multiple times. Now, he had very little he could offer to his visiting kinfolk in the way of hospitality.[349]

Despite the ever-present reminders of war, Elder enjoyed his brief stay with his family. That night, he recorded in his diary: "Said Mass & spent the day very happily." He did the same the following morning and was happy to see his entire family receive Communion.[350]

Immediately after, he set out for nearby Jackson, Louisiana, where he performed some baptisms at a Creole house along the way, and he arrived at Father John Scollard's house at 8:30 in the evening. The two clerics discussed a few administrative matters when they awoke in the morning, then the bishop was on his way back to Woodville, Mississippi. Luckily, he was able to take a train for the last eighteen miles of the journey and arrived in Woodville around six o'clock. Upon his arrival, he was handed a packet of letters. One of them would change the course of the war for the bishop of Natchez, for it would recast the universal struggle between the Catholic Church and secular governments into the template of the Civil War.

JUNE 26 TO AUGUST 13, 1864

SPECIAL ORDERS NO. 31
Provost Marshal's Office
Natchez, Miss., June 28, 1864
Extract - II The Colonel Commanding this District, having been officially notified that the Pastors of many Churches in this city neglect to make any public recognition of allegiance to the Government under which they live, and to which they are indebted for protection; and further, that the regular form of prayer for "The President of the United States and all others in authority," prescribed by the ritual in some Churches, and by established custom in others, has been omitted in the stated services of Churches of all denominations, it is hereby ORDERED that hereafter, the Ministers of such Churches as may have the prescribed form of prayer for the President of the United States, shall read the same at each and every Service in which it is required by the rubrics; and that those of other denominations which have such form, shall on like occasions, pronounce a prayer appropriate to the times and expressive of a proper spirit toward the CHIEF MAGISTRATE OF THE UNITED STATES.
Any Minister failing to comply with these orders will be immediately prohibited from exercising the functions of his office in this city, and render himself liable to be sent beyond the lines of the United States forces, at the discretion of the Colonel Commanding.
The Provost Marshal is charged with the execution of this order.

By Command of B. G. FARRAR (Signed) Colonel Commanding
Jas. E. Montgomery, Ass't Adjt. Gen.
(Official) G. D. Reynolds, Major and Provost Marshal

Natchez, June 28 - 4t

Elder spent the next several days in Woodville after he received notification of Special Order No. 31. He visited parishioners, heard confessions, said Mass, prepared candidates for confirmation and baptized a child. He even spent one afternoon with Amanda Jane "Mary" Bradford, the sister of Confederate president Jefferson Davis. (Mary was buried near her birthplace in Trappist, Kentucky, in the Cistercian monastery, the burial site of the future St. Thomas Merton.) Mary Bradford attended Mass and received Communion from the bishop.[351]

Elder returned to Mrs. Norton's house on Thursday, June 30. He learned that Federal colonel B.G. Farrar, in Natchez, wanted to speak with him about Special Order No. 31 before Mass the next Sunday. Elder knew that he could no longer put off the fateful meeting. The fuse on the powder keg was rapidly burning toward the wick.[352]

The bishop set off for Natchez at once. He arrived that afternoon around 5:30. His urgency was futile, for Colonel Farrar had gone out on an expedition. Instead, Elder met with Captain Montgomery and agreed to remain in Natchez until Colonel Farrar returned in about a week.[353]

That Sunday, Bishop Elder preached Mass "as usual." He gave a homily on the "nature and obligation of an Oath." It was an interesting choice for a homily. Recently, a number of Catholics who had taken an oath of allegiance to the United States had been arrested for smuggling goods out of Natchez and aiding the Confederacy. The bishop was concerned that some of his parishioners were taking their oaths lightly. The bishop tried to rectify this misunderstanding. It is noteworthy that the bishop of Natchez, Mississippi—a stalwart supporter of his flock and their home, which was now his home—would urge his fellow Catholic Confederates to honor their oaths of allegiance to the occupying Federal government. However, Bishop Elder, like all U.S. bishops, North and South, was a firm believer in social stability, and he understood oath-breaking to be amongst the most serious sins, for if men could not trust one another, social chaos and anarchy would become the norm.[354]

Elder's diary entry the following Monday is as interesting as the subject of his homily the previous day. It simply reads: "July 4th Monday. Rain."

Although the day before, the bishop had urged his congregation to honor their oaths and embrace the Union, he must have been torn inside. On July 4, one would expect some notation regarding the most important and patriotic day in his nation's history. Instead, he wrote next to nothing. Certainly, "the Fourth of July" now had a different connotation. After all, it was on July 4, 1863, that Vicksburg had fallen after an excruciating forty-seven-day siege. Now, on July 4, 1864, memories of the devastation he had seen in the aftermath of the siege and in Jackson, Yazoo City and cities all over his diocese flooded Elder's mind. Simply put, there was no longer any joy in the events of eighty-eight years ago. Then, Americans had declared independence and overthrown Great Britain. Now, the South had declared independence and been trampled. Instead of celebratory joy, there was "Rain."[355]

On Wednesday, July 6, Elder and Father Grignon went to Colonel Farrar's headquarters to discuss Special Order No. 31. Although the bishop found the colonel to be polite and hospitable, he could not make the officer understand why he could not say the prayer for President Lincoln during Mass. Colonel Farrar kept insisting that other churches in the state had acquiesced to the Federal demand. Elder insisted that just because others had submitted to an injustice did not mean that he was required to follow suit. When he realized he was at an impasse, Elder asked Farrar if he could submit his reasons for refusing the order in a letter. The colonel asked for time to consider this proposal and told the bishop that he would have an answer by two o'clock that afternoon.[356]

The Bishop was back at Colonel Farrar's at two o'clock. Farrar told Elder that he could write the letter, and he (Farrar) would pass it on to General Henry Slocum. In the meantime, however, Elder would be required to recite the prayer. The bishop told Farrar in no uncertain terms that he would not recite the prayer. In fact, he asked the colonel to go ahead and inform him of his punishment. Farrar, likely stunned by the impertinence—if not the courage—of this bishop who dared refuse the order to which other Christian clerics had already bowed, was at a loss as to what to do. He did nothing. The colonel agreed to let the matter rest until he received orders from General Slocum. Elder emerged from the meeting a free man—at least for the time being.[357]

One week later, Elder finished a nineteen-page letter explaining his refusal to obey Special Order No. 31. He had a parishioner make a copy of the letter for his own records, then he personally took it to Colonel Farrar. However, upon his arrival, he learned that the colonel had been relieved of his duties. Therefore, Elder took the letter to his replacement, Brigadier General

Mason Brayman. Brayman was a Yankee hero, undoubtedly brave in battle, and a bit eccentric, too. He was in the midst of growing an impressive beard that would soon after reach his waist; his patience with Confederates was not so long. Elder described this first encounter with General Brayman:

> *I presented the letter to Brig. Genl. M. Brayman, the new Commander:— an old man—with white hair combed back. He spoke civilly enough:—but he seems to have an idea that everybody that opposes him in any thing must be a bitter rebel. He said he did not approve of men being compelled to read prayers against their conscience: but rather "if he found that we (Fr. Grignon & I) were rebels 'he should treat us as such.'"—He laid the paper down & said he would consider it. He enquired about the Prayer: & I promised to send him the Roman Missal in English.*[358]

Elder left the meeting confident that the reasonableness of his refusal, along with his lengthy explanatory letter, would end favorably for him and his church.

Three days later, his confidence was dashed. While eating his midday meal, the bishop received a letter from General Brayman stating that the general would not bother to reply to his letter. There was no need to: "Military Orders must be obeyed and not discussed."[359]

Brayman's response seemed to settle the matter. There would be no more discussing, justifying, arguing or pleading. Elder was now presented with a clear-cut choice: obey or dissent, acquiesce or be punished.

The remainder of Saturday, July 16, 1864, became Bishop Elder's personal Gethsemane. After living in an occupied state for more than a year, and having seen the horrors of war and the sorrowful consequences of a failing rebellion, Elder understood that the penalty for disobeying the conquerors would be swift and severe. After all, his own brother had been arrested and imprisoned for far less. In fact, his brother had been arrested with no charges whatsoever. Now, Bishop Elder was contemplating disobeying a direct order. That evening, he wrote in his diary:

> *For a while this unnerved me a good deal. I saw the contest was coming to a point—which I had always hoped to avoid. But it was not of my seeking—nor did it concern my private interest—but the interest of religion, the liberty of the Church, & the general liberty of conscience for the whole country. It was clear that I had nothing else to do but oppose a passive resistance, — & leave the consequences to God.*[360]

Bishop Elder did not lightly come to his decision to defy the Federal authorities. Rather, he privately dropped the matter for a time and allowed himself to calm down in the hope that reason would show him the proper course. He also spent much time in prayer trying to discern the will of God. When he said Mass, he offered up the sacrifice for heavenly guidance. He even asked those closest to him and those he most respected to intercede with God on his behalf. "Every light that I could obtain from every quarter had strengthened my conviction of the duty that I owed to God, & to the Church." Elder knew the course he must take—refuse to obey Special Order No. 31—and resolved to follow through on his well-discerned intention.[361]

But then, the doubts came flooding in.

> *Now, I must confess, when the issue was at hand & the prospect of a guard seizing the Cathedral tomorrow or Monday—turning it into a hospital or barracks,—defacing & desecrating everything beautiful & holy—carrying off the most sacred vessels—driving all the Priests out of the house & leaving the people without Sacraments or religious consolation—I must confess the sight of these awful consequences, depending probably on my single word—it did unnerve me. For a few minutes a severe pain shot across the top of my head—& I feared I was going to have a sharp attack of sickness.*[362]

Elder was tempted to renege on his bold intention, to cave in and recite the Federal prayers at Mass, to trample on his conscience.

Then, he was strengthened. He reviewed his motives one final time, spoke with his trusted friend Father Grignon and once more placed the problem before God. "I could only come again to the same conclusion, that to yield, would be for me to do a grievous injury to religion."[363]

With his mind finally at peace, Bishop Elder picked up pen and paper and informed General Brayman of his decision. He asked the general if he intended to disrupt Sunday Mass in the morning. If so, then Elder would accept the consequences, but would make it a simple rather than a High Mass. The bishop wanted as minimal a scene as possible should Brayman decide to arrest him on the spot.[364]

A friend and parishioner, Mr. O'Cavanagh, took the letter to General Brayman. The general intended to ignore the letter, but O'Cavanagh insisted on a response, and Brayman agreed to give him one by 8:30 that night.[365]

Elder eagerly awaited Brayman's response. He got it right at 8:30 p.m. The general told the bishop that he must take sides in the morning. Should he say

An aged Father Mathurin Grignon. *Archives of the Diocese of Jackson.*

the prayer for Lincoln, he would align himself with the United States. Should he refuse, he would side with the Confederacy and be treated as a conquered enemy, a rebel bishop, a secesh prisoner. Brayman, however, did not answer Elder's query; would he be arrested in the morning, during Mass?[366]

After discussing Brayman's response with Father Grignon and two trusted parishioners, Elder decided to go ahead with a High Mass in the morning. He was gambling that Brayman would not want to cause a scene.[367]

On Sunday, July 17, 1864, Elder said Mass at St. Mary's Cathedral. Elder chose to deflect the attention from his situation and instead gave a homily on St. Vincent de Paul. The Bishop finished the Mass—sans prayers for President Lincoln—without any disturbance and left the cathedral a free man.[368]

The following morning, Elder invited a number of prominent citizens, Catholic and Protestant, to his library in order to explain his recent actions.

> *Some Catholics & many more Protestants, were under the impression that my refusal to read the Prayer arises from a preference which I give to the Southern Confederacy.—I wanted them to understand that it was not so— but simply from an unwillingness to acknowledge the right in any secular power to direct our religious worship:—& my own especial unwillingness to use my sacred ministry in maintaining either power or in support of any political views.*[369]

With his stance now known to the Federal authorities and his own townsmen, the meeting adjourned, and Elder awaited the outcome of his rebellion.

He didn't have to wait long. General Brayman sent him a letter in the early afternoon asking the bishop if he had read the prayer for Lincoln. The proverbial ice was beginning to crack beneath the bishop's feet.[370]

The next morning, Elder said Mass for the Sisters of Mercy and went to call upon General Napoleon Jackson Tecumseh Dana. The bishop was praying for a sympathetic ear and was hoping to find one in the Maryland-born General Dana, whose father had been a deathbed convert to Catholicism. Instead, Elder found Captain Eustace in Dana's room. The bishop unloaded his problems upon the sympathetic captain and asked his advice. Captain Eustace sympathized with Elder but said he, unfortunately, had no influence on the case. He explained to Elder that General Brayman was neither a bad man nor an unreasonable man. In fact, he personally opposed Special Order No. 31, but because he was a strict disciplinarian, he intended to see the order obeyed. If he knew what was best for him, Elder would acquiesce.[371]

The entire conversation with Captain Eustace—not to mention every conversation he'd had with the Union brass concerning Special Order No. 31—left Bishop Elder exasperated: "I was struck with the evidence of how entirely the Military spirit has taken possession of these officers, & how thoroughly that spirit abolishes all considerations of any right or claim which may come in conflict with it." It seemed to Elder that a good number of the Union officers sided with him but were of the mindset that orders were orders, all else be damned.[372]

General Dana finally arrived and told Elder that he should have submitted to the order and then asked for a reprieve. Elder replied that such a course of action would have been an acknowledgment of the government's right to control church services. The principle of freedom of conscience and of worship would have been compromised. Dana offered still more sympathy but little help. He did, however, suggest that Elder write a letter to Brayman asking for the injunction to be delayed until both general and bishop received word from Washington, D.C. Dana even offered to take the letter to Brayman himself. With limited options, Elder agreed to take Dana's advice. He went home and wrote a letter to General Brayman in which he admitted to not reciting the prayer at Mass and asking that the penalty for failing to do so be suspended until they received a response from Washington.

The next morning, Elder gathered all his correspondence regarding Special Order No. 31 and sent it to Secretary of War Edwin S. Stanton. The rest of the week passed peacefully, and Elder did not hear from Brayman.[373]

On Monday, July 25, Elder finally learned of his fate. A Federal officer brought him the news, officially labeled Order No. 11. He was now a prisoner of the Union army. The bishop was to go into exile across the river in Vidalia, Louisiana, and there, separated from his diocese, await his fate.[374]

Elder spent the rest of the day preparing for his move and making what arrangements he could to ensure that the diocese would be taken care of during his indefinite exile. He packed his bags; visited with the sisters, whom he tried, in vain, to cheer up; and went to a meeting of the trustees of D'Evereux Hall to clear up some financial questions.[375]

The morning of July 26 was difficult for Elder. For two days, he had been receiving visitors who came to pay their respects to the bishop who was being sent into exile in his own land. "The Sisters & all the Orphans came. Their sobs unmanned me more than anything else." Many more, Catholic and Protestant, were waiting for Elder where the ferry awaited him at Under-the-Hill. As Bishop Elder stepped onto the ferry, he turned around to bid farewell. What he saw greatly moved him. Nearly everyone standing on the bank had fallen to their knees "in the sand & dust," asking for a final blessing from their bishop. That night, Elder lamented in his diary: "God forgive me for not doing my duty better by such a people!"[376]

Elder received an enigmatic welcome when he arrived at his new prison/home. The commanding officer in Vidalia, Colonel Hubert A. McCaleb, seemed uncertain as to the status of his prisoner. He told Elder he could move about freely but must remain inside Union lines, and certainly on the Louisiana side of the river. He further forbade the bishop to write any letters that did not first go through Colonel McCaleb. The colonel then handed over the bishop to a subordinate, who led Elder to his new quarters at the local hotel.[377]

Colonel McCaleb arrived at the hotel a few hours later and informed Elder that he must pay his own expenses. Stunned, Elder, not wanting to impose on his diocese, and seeing the absurdity of the demand, asked McCaleb what would happen if he refused to pay. The colonel told Elder that he would then be taken elsewhere, possibly to a jail cell. Elder then asked McCaleb to make that threat in writing, which the colonel refused to do, stating that he could do as he pleased with his prisoner. Elder suggested that he get in touch with General Brayman and see if the general had a prison cell in mind when he sent the bishop into exile. Colonel McCaleb then changed his tune and told Elder he would find lodging for him and give him soldiers' rations. Elder countered by suggesting that he save money for the government by staying at the home of a local Catholic family, the McDowells. The disgruntled colonel said he would consider it, but in the meantime, he put the bishop in a boardinghouse for the night.[378]

The next afternoon, Elder was informed that he would not receive lodging or rations at the government's expense and must provide for himself. However, he would not be allowed to lodge in town with the McDowells, as Mr. McDowell was currently being investigated on an undisclosed charge.[379]

That first Saturday in Vidalia was depressing for the exiled bishop. He said Mass in a small room with poor accoutrements. He wrote in his diary: "A poor Altar & a poor room for Our Lord. Oh! that I only loved Him as I ought to do for His infinite condescensions." The "Holy Sacrifice" of the Mass had truly become a sacrifice for Bishop Elder, but he knew it was his earthly duty and completed the church's most important prayer—but without the prayer for President Lincoln, the recital of which would have immediately allowed for his release from captivity.[380]

That afternoon, Elder finished a letter to Secretary of War Stanton and delivered it, per instructions, to Colonel McCaleb for review. Also that afternoon, Colonel McCaleb informed Elder that he now had permission to lodge with the McDowells during his exile.[381]

As soon as Elder awoke the next morning, Sunday, July 31, he went straight to the McDowells' house. Mrs. McDowell covered her piano with a tablecloth, turning it into an altar so the bishop could say Mass. Elder spent the next twelve days with the McDowells and enjoyed his prison sentence as much as any prisoner could. He entertained a constant stream of visitors from Natchez, who brought him and his hosts what daily comforts they could. The bishop recorded his general impressions of his time at the McDowells.

> But more than bodily comforts, was the kindness of the sympathy shown by the many who came to visit me; & the many others who could not come, but who sent kind messages—& the many others still who did all in their power for me by their fervent prayers; in Natchez, Vicksburgh, New Orleans & every where.[382]

Elder said Mass in a much better mood that Sunday morning, then visited the hospitals in Vidalia.[383]

The following day, Monday, August 1, 1864, was the feast day of St. Peter in Chains. This feast commemorated the deliverance of St. Peter, the direct spiritual predecessor of Bishop Elder and all Catholic bishops, from the chains in which King Herod bound him—this had taken place eighteen centuries before Elder himself was bound in metaphorical chains by another secular authority. That same day, Father Grignon received his own letter from General Brayman asking if he had recited the prayer for President Lincoln. It appeared as if Father Grignon would soon be joining his bishop in exile.[384]

The following Thursday, Father Grignon, taking over his bishop's duties in Natchez, visited General Brayman, and he gave the general the same answer Elder had given nearly two weeks earlier. Ominously, Brayman replied as he had to Elder: he would get back to him later.[385]

That afternoon, Father Grignon's presence was requested by a sick Federal soldier at the Marine Hospital. The priest went straight to the hospital but was stopped along the way and sent back. Evidently, his pass, signed by General Brayman, had expired. The priest went back to his rectory, and the Union soldier was left without consolation. Parishioner Joseph Arrighi offered to renew the pass for Father Grignon. The generous parishioner took the request to General Brayman's residence. He made his request and sent the pass into the general's room in the care of a subordinate officer. Shortly after, the officer returned, tore the pass into pieces and threw it into the fireplace, exclaiming: "The general desires me to say to you that

Father Mathurin Grignon, vicar general of the Diocese of Natchez. *Archives of the Diocese of Jackson.*

he is neither renewing passes nor giving them." The stunned parishioner walked back and reported the bizarre episode to Father Grignon. Not long after, Father Grignon received an urgent plea from the Marine Hospital: the Federal soldier who had requested his presence was now beside himself and was threatening to throw himself from a window if Father Grignon did not arrive soon.

Father Grignon was granted a one-day pass to visit the hospital the following afternoon. However, he did not receive it until late in the afternoon. When he arrived at the hospital to visit the distressed soldier, he found six or seven other needy Catholic soldiers. The distraught priest did for them what he could with the short amount of time allotted to him.[386]

Bishop Elder spent the following Sunday, August 10, still confined in Vidalia. Again, he received many visitors from Natchez bearing sympathy, greetings, news and gifts. Elder tried to use some of these gifts to pay the McDowells for their generosity, but Mrs. McDowell would have none of it. When Elder was insistent, she told him that if he felt he must pay something, he should give it to the orphans. That is what Elder did. The next day, the bishop received a very welcome surprise—a few of the sisters crossed the river and brought the littlest of his beloved orphans to visit him.[387]

Father Mathurin Grignon, who very nearly joined his bishop in exile when he, too, refused to include a prayer for Abraham Lincoln during Mass. *Archives of the Diocese of Jackson.*

On Wednesday, August 12, Elder was sitting with Mrs. McDowell, her mother and another parishioner when he received a letter from General Brayman that suspended his exile until word should come from Washington. In addition, he would not be required to say the prayer for President Lincoln until the matter was settled. Naturally, Elder was elated and began immediate preparations to return to his see in Natchez.[388]

The bishop left that day for the ferry that would return him to freedom and duty. Along the way, he stopped to baptize a four-year-old girl in Vidalia who was dying of dropsy. He then boarded the ferry and crossed the river. He disembarked at Under-the-Hill and rode back to his house with two loyal parishioners. As he traversed the streets of Natchez, more and more people recognized him and realized the bishop had returned. Upon arriving at his house, he saw a small crowd already gathered, and he immediately made his way to the church to give thanks. Upon his arrival, the bells began to ring, and crowds of grateful parishioners began to arrive at both the rectory and St. Mary's. That evening, Elder recorded the joy of the day in his diary:

St. Mary's Catholic Orphanage for Girls, Natchez, Mississippi. *Archives of the Diocese of Jackson.*

> *What fervent thanks to God, what joyous congratulations to me.—I gave full scope to my joy. Personally I had endured no suffering. But I had seriously feared the dreadful consequences of desecrating the Church, & perhaps banishing all the Priests as the Order had declared. So that there was truly great reason for rejoicing that the cloud had passed & done no harm,*[389]

Elder credited prayer, particularly the intercession of Mary, for bringing about an end to his exile and, more importantly, for preserving the freedom of the universal church. He was also careful to give temporal credit to Federal adjutant general Lorenzo Thomas, who had been in Natchez a few days earlier and interceded on Elder's behalf, as well as a few Natchez citizens who had taken his case to General Thomas.[390]

It is noteworthy that Bishop Elder gave no credit for the suspension of his sentence to General Brayman. In fact, in his diary, he condemns the general for the hypocritical wording of the reprieving order. He hints that Brayman was releasing him only to please General Thomas: "If there were any opening for me to express my thanks I shd. be glad to do so. The wording of the Order effectually precludes it." Elder was reasonably justified in his bitterness toward Brayman, for the general does seem to have been overruled by a higher authority. Brayman's letter to the bishop concludes:

> *And as all solemn appeals to the Supreme Being, not proceeding from honest hearts, and willing minds, are necessarily offensive to Him, and subversive of sound morality, so much of Special Order No. 31, June 18, 1864, as requires public prayer to be pronounced, in behalf of the President of the United States, and the Union, is suspended until further orders; leaving all persons conducting Divine Worship, at liberty to manifest such measure of hostility, as they may feel, against the Government of the Union of these States, and their sympathy with the rebellion, by omitting such supplication, if so minded.*[391]

The wording of the letter certainly hints that Bishop Elder, and all others who refused to offer prayers to President Lincoln, were subversive rebels deserving of whatever punishment their conquerors imposed. Elder never expressed his gratitude to General Brayman.

The morning after Bishop Elder returned to his diocese, he paid a visit to the orphans he had been forced to leave behind—their spiritual father had returned, and he spent the day amongst the least of his flock.[392]

AUGUST 14 TO DECEMBER 27, 1864

Elder's first Sunday homily after his return to Natchez was politically and socially significant, as well as a fine glimpse into the soul of the bishop. The assigned liturgical Gospel reading for the day was the story of Jesus and the healing of the ten lepers—some Jews, some Samaritans. Elder purposefully failed to mention the political events of the last week—his own exile and the treatment of Father Grignon. Instead, he promised to remember all those who had been fervently praying for him—and his cause—over the last couple of weeks; he would offer his next Mass for them. He then proceeded to explain the significance of the Sunday Gospel: Jews and Samaritans, political enemies, now united, begged a boon of their one Lord. They represented healing, a cessation to divisiveness, a common cause. Bishop Elder now longed for a similar attitude among his flock. And his flock was neither Federal nor Confederate, Catholic nor Protestant, black nor white, but mankind. As Elder himself wrote in his diary that night, "the Catholic Church wishes friends & enemies to unite before the same altar & say prayers common to all."[393]

The next day, Elder again said Mass, this time on behalf of the Feast of the Assumption of Mary. The bishop took the time to express his belief that the recent events demonstrated the intercessory power of the Blessed Virgin Mary, as well as her affection for the persons of the Diocese of Natchez. That evening, he heard from Mrs. Arrighi. Her nephew, Mr. Buckley, had

Yellow Jack. Library of Congress.

died that night in her house. She and the doctor told the bishop the ominous news: he died of yellow fever.

The next week and a half passed as usual for wartime occupied Natchez. Elder said Mass, gave a retreat for the sisters, began another retreat for confirmation and first Communion applicants, and got embroiled in another church-state dispute—or rather, a church-Brayman dispute.[394]

Father Grignon asked for a pass to visit Federal soldiers in the Federal hospital. True to his actions of the past month, General Brayman told the priest, "maybe." If Brayman decided to send the pass, he would; if not, he wouldn't. Father Grignon waited the rest of the day for the pass. He then waited through the next day. Finally, Bishop Elder decided to pay his respects to General Thomas. He recorded his impressions of the general that night in his diary:

> *I had learned on good authority that he it was that obtained my recall. He received me very pleasantly. He seems to be a reasonable & a kind man. I told him of the refusal of the pass to visit the sick soldiers. He expressed his surprise and dislike: said he could not directly interfere but he would speak to the Commander.*[395]

At least in the eyes of Bishop Elder, General Thomas was a much easier man to deal with than General Brayman. Although Brayman was still the official commandant of Natchez, Adjutant General Thomas sometimes acted as an arbiter between Elder and Brayman.

Two days later, General Thomas offered Elder his interpretation of General Brayman's behavior. Thomas believed that Brayman's feelings had been hurt when the cathedral bells rang at the bishop's return. He thought Elder was making a fool of him and rubbing in the fact that he was now home—against the general's wishes. The bishop went home after trying to explain the difference between joy and revenge and that his parishioners had been expressing the former when they rang the cathedral bells.[396]

The next week seemed an extension of every week since General Brayman had replaced Colonel Farrar as commandant of Natchez in mid-July. Elder applied to the general for a pass to visit the hospitals. He was told he would receive an answer the following day. He went back the next afternoon and was told to come back the next day. It was not ready the next day, nor the next, nor the next. Finally, five days after applying for permission to visit sick Union soldiers, Elder wrote to the previously sympathetic General Dana for a pass.[397]

Ten days later, Bishop Elder was still waiting for a pass to visit the hospitalized Federal soldiers. In the meantime, he said Mass, visited the orphanage, anointed the dying, visited the smallpox hospital and went back to Vidalia a few times, most notably to visit Mrs. Tipton, the mother of Mrs. McDowell, with whom he had lodged during his exile.[398]

In fact, the rest of September and October passed in much the same manner as the occupation began to settle into normalcy. There were Masses, hospital visits, baptisms, run-ins with Union officials and the usual monotony mixed with the moments of excitement that most lives offer. One interesting occurrence happened at Sunday Mass on October 16, 1864. Bishop Elder noted that evening in his diary that he had said the Mass unaccompanied by the organ. His usual organist, Mary Hollingsworth, had resigned. She had been performing at Sunday services at St. Mary's for some time despite being a devout Episcopalian. This arrangement was highly unusual in this age of dogmatism and separation—there was little spirit of ecumenism between the Christian churches in the mid-nineteenth century. However, Hollingsworth was disappointed that her own Episcopal pastor was reciting prayers for President Lincoln during services. Therefore, she offered her services to the Catholic church. Now that the controversial prayer was no longer required to be given in Natchez, Hollingsworth gratefully returned to her preferred (and now, in her mind, untainted) Episcopal church.[399]

November 1864 began as October had ended. Masses, baptisms, last rites, funerals. Interestingly, the Masses were of the Low variety, because "the choir is out of harmony & out of wind—no organist." Of course, there were the usual encounters with Federal authorities who had decided it was time for a severe crackdown on disloyal former Confederate citizens. A number of Elder's parishioners in Natchez received yet another blow to their pocketbooks and pride. Dominic Arrighi was forced to enlist in the newly organized Federal militia or else get the necessary exemption papers.[400] Mrs. Perrault was informed that her house would be taken over by the Federal government. Even church property suffered under this new crackdown. The cemetery fence, which Union general Marcellus Crocker had already repaired once, was again torn down.[401]

Near the end of November, Antonio Genella of Vicksburg procured a pass for the bishop to visit Vicksburg. The pass was signed by General Napoleon J.T. Dana and was good for sixty days. Two days later, Elder was on a boat headed north. Interestingly, he was approached just before boarding by a man named Nutterville, who spoke amiably with the bishop. Elder believed him to have been a parishioner whose name had drifted from his memory.

He was probably one of those Catholics who attended Mass at his own will rather than God's. After all, churches tended to be much more crowded on Easter and Christmas than during other times. However, once he boarded the boat, Elder was informed by a fellow traveler that the "parishioner" Nutterville was actually a detective. Clearly, the bishop's loyalty was still being questioned.[402]

The morning after his arrival in Vicksburg, Elder said Mass, then visited the Sisters of Mercy at their convent. The nuns were in the midst of conducting classes and had a large contingent of boys and girls in attendance. The bishop was pleased. He was convinced that his diocese needed as much normalcy as possible during these difficult times. He was also convinced of the necessity of educating and protecting the future of his diocese. With so many of his flock buried on distant battlefields or perishing at home for want of food, medicine or doctors, he took it upon himself to serve and shepherd those whom he could. It would be these young Mississippians, many of them orphans, who would lead the state and his diocese in the painful decades to come.[403]

Elder was pleased to learn that General Dana had been exceedingly kind to the sisters. The nuns had been staying with Major Jared and Minerva Cook at their plantation, Hard Times, outside the city. General Dana sent some wagons to the house to bring the sisters' furniture back to their convent. He also donated some lumber to repair their damaged fence. A few days later, Elder paid his respects to the Federal general who had been so kind to his nuns. He also asked General Dana if some of his priests could receive passes to travel between the lines. He explained that he was responsible for those souls inside Vicksburg as well as those inside Confederate lines—and everyone in between. The general said he was sure he could procure the necessary passes.[404]

Pleased with his journey to Vicksburg, particularly with the state of the Catholic schools, Bishop Elder boarded the *Gray Eagle* and returned to Natchez. He arrived on the evening of December 2 and found that Father Grignon had not been doing well physically while the bishop was in Vicksburg. Elder, therefore, said both Masses in the morning and prayed that his loyal and trusted priest would shortly recover.[405]

Elder spent the next several days, from morning until night, conducting a retreat for the orphaned girls of the asylum.[406] When the retreat concluded on December 11, the Feast of the Immaculate Conception, Elder completed the final two weeks of Advent, performing his usual pastoral duties.[407]

Christmas Day arrived. It had rained hard the previous night and was still raging in the morning, when Elder and a still sick Father Grignon arose to say Mass. Father Grignon did what he could to assist his bishop, but it was up to Elder to preach at both Masses. He said another Mass the next morning at the orphanage before departing for Vicksburg on the boat *Joseph Pierce*. Twenty-four hours later, Elder was back in Vicksburg, where he would spend the next six weeks.[400]

20

THE OCCUPATION

The citizens were on edge. The unthinkable had happened. The "Gibraltar of the West" now flew a Union flag. The city was occupied by enemy troops.

However, as long as General Joe Johnston still held the eastern half of the state, as long as Nathan Bedford Forrest rode free and, most importantly, as long as Robert E. Lee was still confounding Yankee troops in Virginia, there was hope. One day, hopefully sooner than later, Vicksburg would be free and would once again fly the Stars and Bars above its courthouse. Until then, the conquered but unvanquished would have to grit their teeth and endure a humiliating occupation.

The world they had known had been turned upside down. Those still in Vicksburg—whether rich or poor, man or woman, black or white—were living in strange and dangerous times. President Abraham Lincoln had suspended habeas corpus, making all citizens, rebel and Unionist alike, liable to be arrested at the slightest provocation or, in some cases, no provocation at all. Five women had been exiled from the city and thrown at the mercy of the dangerous and unsettled landscape outside Vicksburg. Their crime: walking out of Christ's Episcopal Church when the minister offered up prayers for Abraham Lincoln rather than Jefferson Davis. All were requested to sign an oath of allegiance. Those who refused were harassed and placed under surveillance. One slip-up would lead to a massive fine or a prison sentence. The Union commanders swore in former slaves to serve as patrollers. Those who had fled to the caves to

Robert E. Lee.
Metropolitan Museum of Art.

escape the myriad and dangerous shells during the siege had their property declared abandoned and then confiscated.[409]

As the shock of defeat finally sank in during the days and weeks following Confederate general John C. Pemberton's surrender on July 4, 1863, the citizens of Vicksburg shifted from fearing death by cannonball to fretting over how to survive the confiscation of their property, possessions and food. Their anger simmered over wanton acts of destruction, losing their rights as citizens and having to see the Yankees everywhere. But undoubtedly, the most frustrating aspect of the occupation to most residents of Vicksburg was the incessant bureaucracy. The lines, the waiting, the paperwork, the shifting around, the new lines, more waiting and more paperwork took its toll on the people. They all experienced it. If anything, the capture of Vicksburg democratized the city in a way no one could have foreseen.

The citizens were forced to rely on the Federal government for food rations. The lines were long and required a lot of paperwork. When they finally got to the front of the line, they were given five days' rations. The Union physician Seneca B. Throll described how food passes worked:

> *A citizen goes to one officer and gets a "provision return," he takes it to another officer to have it approved and an order to issue the rations endorsed upon it. Then to another building to a clerk, who takes the provision return and estimates the number of pounds due of meat, coffee, sugar, flour, etc. Upon the return, gives a ticket, which is then taken to the issuing clerk who finally, when your turn comes, gives you "five days rations."*[410]

The process, of course, would have to be repeated every five days, and five days after that, for as long as the war—or at least the occupation—continued.

A.B. Reading was a railroad entrepreneur who lived on a large plantation and owned a foundry and two cotton gins. He waited in the food line like everyone else. Candie Newman was a free black woman. She owned a good-sized dairy. The fact that she was a Union sympathizer did not protect her from the confiscation of her cattle. She, too, had to wait in the long lines for her five-day ration. Ida Luckett was raising her grandchildren. Their father—her son-in-law—had been killed in battle fighting for the Confederacy. Federal troops came and took all her cattle and possessions, wagonload by wagonload. They even took all her eggs. "As she watched the work of a lifetime wiped away in an afternoon, she sobbed and wrung her hands and then turned and went inside. Destitute and hungry with not enough food for the family, she left most of what she had for the children." The Lucketts, too, would soon be standing in line waiting for food.[411]

Even under these circumstances, the Lucketts were the lucky ones. On May 18, 1864, as Bishop Elder was dining with Dr. O'Leary in Canton,[412] John H. Bobb heard a noise in his garden. Almost immediately, he saw several Union troops rummaging through his flowers. Incensed, he told them to leave. When they refused, Bobb picked up a brick and hurled it at one of the offending soldiers. Bobb then marched straight to General Slocum's headquarters to report the incident. As he returned home, Federal troops arrested him, took him to the nearby railroad yard and shot him dead. Just like that—no trial, no formal charge, just a bullet that ended his life.

When General Slocum heard of the incident, he sent an officer to investigate. The officer found Selina Bobb weeping over the body of her still-warm but motionless husband.[413]

DECEMBER 27, 1864, TO MARCH 27, 1865

E lder began his Vicksburg sojourn by giving a retreat to the Sisters of Mercy who wished to renew their vows. He also oversaw the final profession of one young lady who took the name Sister Philomena. The newest sister entered the ranks of the Sisters of Mercy on New Year's Day, 1865.[414]

Bishop Elder spent the next two weeks doing the usual pastoral duties of a parish priest. Once again, the administrative head of the diocese was forced to join the ranks of his diminishing number of clerics and help them in the field. He said Masses. He taught catechism. He performed baptisms. He heard confessions—lots of confessions. "During all this week & for several weeks after—I was much occupied with Confessions….Heard Confession every morning after Mass." Evidently, the war was forcing his parishioners to contemplate their own mortality.[415]

Elder suffered another blow on January 10, 1865, when he allowed one of his finest priests, Father Charles Heuze, to leave his diocese and join the contemplative order of Marists. Father Heuze had grown increasingly depressed as the war continued. He had been a seminarian in France when Father Grignon made a recruiting tour. The young Heuze was the only man who volunteered his services in Natchez. He arrived at his mission in mid-1860 and was almost immediately ordained. Fate led to him being posted at Vicksburg. The war, the siege and its aftermath caused the overworked priest to slide into a deep depression. He had been asking, then begging, Elder to allow him to join the Marists for some time. Elder knew he needed

Father Heuze's services, but he also empathized with the distraught priest and understood Father Heuze to be one of his sheep. Elder had a duty to care for all members of his flock, priests included. Reluctantly, Bishop Elder gave Father Hueze permission to follow his heart's desire. That evening, the bishop wrote in his diary: "I allowed Fr. Hueze to leave the Missions to go to be a religious among the Marists. It is with great pain. He is most exemplary & zealous—a Missionary invaluable. But he has been begging ever since the siege was over:— & he is really unhappy with the delay."[416]

The bishop's generosity and concern for Father Hueze's damaged psyche cost him another priest. He had already lost Fathers Orlandi, Boheme, Guillou and Elia. Still, the war continued.

While Father Hueze made his way to Lyon, France (and then to Dublin, London and, ultimately, Australia, where he died eighteen years later),[417] life went on as normal in Natchez—at least, it was normal by the standard of the last two years in an occupied town surrounded by ruin and destruction in the midst of a crumbling state. Elder said Masses, performed two more baptisms (as if two more neophytes could replace the countless sheep he had already lost at home and on distant battlefields) and, of course, spent hours in the confessional.[418]

The hectic schedule, and the ordeals of the last four years, were taking a toll on Bishop Elder. On the last day of January 1865, he stayed in bed with severe back pain. He sent for help outside his diocese. Father Charles Van Queckelberge promised to come to his aid from Belgium. Van Queckelberge had been in the United States for two years but had been unable to reach his assignment in Natchez due to the war. However, he had recently told Elder he would shortly be in Natchez—that promise had been made a month earlier. Elder also heard that Father Patrick McCabe from All Hallows, in Dublin, Ireland, had arrived in Natchez. The bishop requested that Father McCabe come to Vicksburg to give him much-needed help. It took five days for Father McCabe to make the journey from Natchez to Vicksburg.[419] Eight months later, Father McCabe died of typhoid fever in Vicksburg.[420]

In the meantime, the rheumatic Elder was forced to perform all priestly functions in Vicksburg. He said both Masses on Sunday, February 5, and then began a tiring and muddy search for someone who had contracted smallpox. It was clear that Elder needed a respite as much as he needed help running his many parishes. Yet he continued to persevere in his vocation, even willing to leave behind the relatively healthy sheep of Vicksburg and seek out the lamb who was lost and suffering in the wilderness.[421]

Help finally came when Father McCabe arrived in Vicksburg on February 8. Elder stayed another week, updating Father McCabe on the situation in Vicksburg, then boarded the *Joseph Pierce* and returned to Natchez.[422]

Elder arrived at his episcopal headquarters on February 15, 1865, and immediately said Mass. Afterward, he went to a fair held on behalf of the orphanage. The bishop was greatly impressed with the fundraiser. He noted that a good number of Protestants were in attendance, including the Reverend Dr. Boyd. Evidently, the war and its inevitable progeny—orphans—were uniting the Christian sects in concern for the vulnerable. Among those in attendance was Major Jared Cook, who was also one of the chief organizers. At the time, the major could not have known his wife, Minerva, would be murdered in just six weeks. The fair lasted for five days and netted $5,643 for the orphanage.[423]

Among those present at the fair was General John Davidson, the new Federal commander at Natchez. Bishop Elder paid a visit to General Davidson during his first week back in Natchez. He found the new commander to be an agreeable man. Davison himself had recently entered the Catholic Church. While he was stationed in California, Davidson witnessed the death of one of his officers and was much impressed with his fortitude. The officer's faith had allowed him to die with confidence. Davidson wanted that same serenity and mettle and was soon baptized. Now in Natchez, the recent convert was waiting to receive his first Communion.[424]

The first week back in Natchez was trying for Bishop Elder. Two of his parishioners died on the same day, February 23. Both died before Elder could reach them and offer last rites. The bishop was emotionally distraught at having lost two men who spent their final moments so close to his residence. Two days later, another parishioner "was killed out in the country." Father Grignon, still sick, presided over the unfortunate man's funeral.

On his first Sunday back in Natchez, Elder wrote in his diary: "Febry. 26th. Sunday—The Bishop alone—had to do all." As the war went on and on, and more and more unfavorably, Bishop Elder pushed himself to his limits. He had little help, and if the war did not end soon, he very well might have a dying Father Grignon preside over his own funeral Mass—that is, assuming Father Grignon outlived him.[425]

The following Saturday, March 4, 1865, proved to be a memorable day for the tired bishop. His two most recent converts were executed for murder. That Friday, Elder had received word that two condemned men were to be executed in the morning. The bishop went to visit the prisoners; while there, he learned that one had been baptized into the Episcopal church that morning. The Episcopal minister, Dr. Perry, had made arrangements with the frightened men to return in the morning and accompany them to their deaths. Elder, believing the men to be provided for, planned to return to his rectory, but the condemned asked that he stay with them. They both wished to receive instruction in the Catholic faith. Elder consented and remained with them until 10:30 that night with only a brief respite to offer prayers for his own congregation.

Elder awoke early the following morning, as was his habit. He drank a cup of coffee and then made his way to the prison. The two prisoners asked the bishop to bring them into the Catholic Church. Not wanting to ruffle any feathers, Elder wrote to Dr. Perry and informed him that the men had asked for admittance into the Church of Rome. He then proceeded to confirm the men and gave them Holy Communion, confirming their status as neophyte Catholics.

Shortly after, Dr. Perry arrived and got on to Elder for stealing his converts. He claimed "prior right" and said that he would be accompanying the two to their execution in just a couple of hours. Elder refused to back down, and fortunately for him, the lieutenant on guard agreed with him—the men clearly wished to die as Catholics under the care of Bishop Elder. They had even made this claim in front of Dr. Perry. However, Dr. Perry was not to be deterred. He took his case to the provost marshal, who quickly ruled in his favor—the condemned would die as members of the Episcopal Church. Elder countered by going directly to his recent acquaintance, General Davidson. Perhaps thinking of the conviction with which his Catholic officer had faced certain death in California, the general ruled that the men be allowed to choose for themselves. If they wished to die in the arms of the faith he himself had just professed, and which his friend had embraced on his deathbed, the general would not stand in the way.

The condemned men chose Catholicism, and Bishop Elder accompanied them to the site where they were to die. Later that night, he wrote: "They were both very penitent—We talked together all the way." The two men Elder had fought for, his two most recent converts, died the day he welcomed them into his church.[426]

After only three weeks in Natchez, Elder was on his way back to Vicksburg, the city that now occupied so much of his time. He arrived on March 7, 1865, and immediately said Mass and organized a retreat for first Communion and confirmation candidates.

The next day, Elder received some of the best news he had heard in quite some time: Father Charles Van Queckelberge had arrived from St.

Louis. The desperately needed priest had tried four times to come to the overextended bishop's aid. Each time he attempted to make the journey, however, he grew seriously sick and had to postpone the trip. Elder "had given up all hopes of his coming" and left Father McCabe to run the large Vicksburg parish by himself. In the meantime, Elder planned to make an odyssey into the interior of the state and bring back one of the priests to serve the Catholics of Vicksburg. Now, the stress of this journey—and the worry about depriving Catholics of the interior of a much needed priest—dissipated. The bishop immediately installed Father Van Queckelberge as pastor of Vicksburg.[427]

Elder received more encouraging news during his first Sunday in Vicksburg. He confirmed 104 new Catholics during that Sunday's Mass. Interestingly, and perhaps with a touch of humor (and an abundance of practicality), Elder noted that evening in his diary that the confirmation candles in church were posing a potential problem. When the newest initiates lit their candles, those wearing veils came dangerously close to setting their veils on fire. The candles also posed a distraction for the young children who were supposed to be following the Mass in their prayer books. Elder suggested the candles be lit at the beginning of the service and extinguished a little while after. Surely, the problem of distracted parishioners and singed veils paled in comparison to the myriad problems that had plagued Elder and his diocese in recent months.[428]

Elder spent the rest of Sunday, March 12, with the Sisters of Mercy and saw all the good they were accomplishing in Vicksburg. The mother superior had already left for Shelby Springs, Alabama, to bring back another sister to help with the order's various projects. Of primary importance to the nuns—now that the war was coming to an end and hospital duties were significantly lightened—was the education of the next generation. Bishop Elder gave his wholehearted support to any educational undertaking in his diocese. Currently, the sisters were constructing a two-story frame schoolhouse. Elder wrote in his diary: "It is wonderful & delightful—what a spirit of piety & zeal the Sisters are giving to the children—& how the children are influencing their Parents—& the other children." He also noted that there were three other Catholic women operating schools in the area and that all four Catholic schools were "in good harmony."[429]

Two days later, Elder was back on the *Joseph Pierce* heading toward Natchez. Aboard the ship, he learned from one of the passengers that there were four orphaned children, all siblings, who were currently staying at the

Sergeant place. Filled with pity, Elder agreed to take all four children into his orphanage in Natchez.[430]

Two weeks and four entries later, Bishop Elder concluded his Civil War diary on March 27, 1865. It was an appropriate time to end the journal. Lee's surrender at Appomattox would occur roughly two weeks later, on April 9. Joe Johnston would surrender his forces in Greensboro, North Carolina, on April 26. The last Confederate force gave up the fight in Texas on June 2, 1865. All of these dates and surrenders were almost a moot point for Elder and his fellow Mississippians, for Mississippi had been a conquered state for the past year. Now, however, the war was officially over.

CONCLUSION

In 1865, the military operations of the Civil War ended. However, the ideological war continued. Slaves were now free. However, they would not truly be free until they won another war—for civil rights—one hundred years later. Mississippi's soldiers—some of them—had returned home. However, they carried emotional and physical scars that would haunt them forever. A state that had produced a worldview that preached the inherent superiority of one race over another had been decisively defeated in war. However, Mississippi was "redeemed" twelve years later by ballot-stuffing, intimidation and terrorism that allowed a new, legal racist regime to operate with impunity for the next century.

The casualty lists, which had been printed with too much regularity in the newspapers, ceased. However, then yellow fever struck and struck again, and the death lists returned. Bishop Elder shepherded his flock through antebellum days, the war, Reconstruction and the yellow fever epidemic.

In the middle of 1865, Bishop Elder's world was turned upside down—or perhaps right side up. The shepherd had prayed that war would never divide his nation. When it came, he prayed for a quick resolution. When a protracted and bloody conflict became inevitable, he chose to serve the sheep with whom he had been entrusted. It ended up being a diverse flock—white people (whether racist, moderate or indifferent), slaves, freedmen and Yankees. His language was a product of his times; his actions were a product of his faith.

Bishop Elder left Natchez for good in 1880, when he was appointed the archbishop of Cincinnati. He served in that capacity until his death in 1904 at age eighty-five. Elder had bridged the gap between the War of 1812 and the advent of World War I. He had been a bishop for nearly fifty years. He had seen more than his fair share of war, destruction, disease and death. Yet, through it all, he continued to teach, preach, minister, baptize, confirm, forgive, marry, comfort and lead. Bishop Elder lived as a pastor to his people—all of his people.

Notes

Chapter 1

1. William Henry Elder, Subject File, Mississippi Department of Archives and History.
2. Ibid.
3. Pastoral letter issued by the Ninth Provincial Council of Baltimore, 1858 quoted in Pillar, *Catholic Church in Mississippi*, 156.
4. Pastoral letter issued by the Third Provincial Council of Cincinnati, May 1861, quoted in Pillar, *Catholic Church in Mississippi*, 157.
5. The mid-eighteenth-century Catholic Church was still heavily influenced by scholasticism, most notably the teachings of Thomas Aquinas, who claimed that a war could be just if certain criteria were met: it must be waged by a proper authority, for a just cause, and peace must be the ultimate aim.
6. Pillar, *Catholic Church in Mississippi*, 157.
7. Ibid.
8. Advent is a season in the Catholic liturgical calendar consisting of the four weeks leading up to Christmas. It is a time of preparation and penance.
9. *New York Tablet* IV, no. 30 (December 22, 1860): 11, quoted in Pillar, *Catholic Church in Mississippi*, 159.
10. Elder to Kenrick, undated fragment, found in a file after a letter dated April 12, 1861. Archives of the Archdiocese of Baltimore, 29-D-12. quoted in Pillar, *Catholic Church in Mississippi*, 160.

11. Elder to Duggan, Natchez, February 19, 1861; Elder Letter Book No. 6, 37 Archives of the Diocese of Jackson, quoted in Pillar, *Catholic Church in Mississippi*, 161.

12. Elder to Kenrick, undated fragment, found in a file after another of Elder's letters dated April 12, 1861, Archives of the Archdiocese of Baltimore, 29-D-12, quoted in Pillar, *Catholic Church in Mississippi*, 161.

13. Elder to Duggan, Natchez, March 5, 1861; Elder Letter Book No. 6, 96 Archives of the Diocese of Jackson, quoted in Pillar, *Catholic Church in Mississippi*, 162–163.

14. Pillar, *Catholic Church in Mississippi*, 167.

Chapter 2

15. Elder, *Civil War Diary*, 1.

16. *Mississippi Free Trader*, April 25, 1859.

17. Ibid.

18. *Natchez Courier*, October 9, 1862.

19. Ibid.

20. *Natchez Daily Courier*, November 18, 1862.

21. Elder, *Civil War Diary*, 5, 19.

Chapter 3

22. Henry Morton Stanley, *The Autobiography of Sir Henry Morton Stanley*, quoted in Groom, *Shiloh*, 269.

23. Augustus Mecklin as quoted in Wynne, *Mississippi's Civil War*, 210.

24. Ibid.

25. Groom, *Shiloh*, 358.

26. Groom, *Shiloh*, 263.

27. Brinsfield, *Faith in the Fight*, 85.

28. "Catholic Priest Killed at Battle of Jonesborough Holds Historical Significance," http://www.news-daily.com/news/catholic-priest-killed-at-battle-of-jonesborough-holds-historical-significance/article_efeadc17-26a2-5eb4-8917-02c6577c32ac.html, accessed June 1, 2018.

29. Stanley, *Autobiography*, quoted in Groom, *Shiloh*, 275.

30. Groom, *Shiloh*, 342.

31. Mecklin quoted in Wynne, *Mississippi's Civil War*, 213.

32. Ibid.

33. Groom, *Shiloh*, 388.
34. Groom, *Shiloh*, 387–88.

Chapter 4

35. Elder, *Civil War Diary*, 2.
36. Ibid.
37. Ibid.
38. The Host is the sacramental bread that Catholics believe turns into the Body of Christ during the Mass. Only Catholics in good standing in the church and with no serious (mortal) sin on their souls may receive the Host. Therefore, it is safe to assume that a person who takes the Host has recently been to the sacrament of Reconciliation.
39. Elder, *Civil War Diary*, 3.
40. Ibid.
41. Elder to Huber, Natchez, October 23, 1862; Elder Letter Book No. 8, 126, Archives of the Diocese of Jackson, quoted in Pillar, *Catholic Church in Mississippi*, 229.
42. Beagle and Giemza, *Poet of the Lost Cause*, 44–47. In 1977, the Diocese of Natchez-Jackson was split in two. The Diocese of Biloxi was created along the Mississippi Gulf Coast. At the time of the Civil War, however, Biloxi was still in Elder's jurisdiction.
43. Elder, *Civil War Diary*, 10; Pillar, *Catholic Church in Mississippi*, 230.
44. Pillar, *Catholic Church in Mississippi*, 230.
45. Elder, *Civil War Diary*, 4.
46. Ibid.
47. Elder, *Civil War Diary*, 5.

Chapter 5

48. Elder, *Character-Glimpses*, 11.
49. Elder, *Character-Glimpses*, 13.
50. Elder, *Character-Glimpses*, 17.
51. Elder, *Character-Glimpses*, 18.
52. Elder, *Character-Glimpses*, 20.
53. Elder, *Character-Glimpses*, 27.
54. Elder, *Character-Glimpses*, 33–34.

Chapter 6

55. Elder, *Civil War Diary*, 5.
56. Elder, *Civil War Diary*, 5–6.
57. Elder, *Civil War Diary*, 6.
58. Elder, *Civil War Diary*, 7.
59. Elder, *Civil War Diary*, 8.
60. Ibid.
61. Elder's church teaches that a soul can be forgiven, but the sins must still be paid for. Because of Kenny's late reconversion, she would be welcomed into heaven but still had to pay for a lifetime of sins. Such penance would be performed in purgatory.
62. Elder, *Civil War Diary*, 9.
63. Ibid.
64. Ibid.
65. Ibid.
66. Elder, *Civil War Diary*, 10.
67. Ibid.
68. Ibid.
69. Elder, *Civil War Diary*, 11.
70. Ibid.
71. Elder, *Civil War Diary*, 12.
72. Ibid.
73. Elder, *Civil War Diary*, 13.
74. Ibid.
75. Ibid.
76. Elder, *Civil War Diary*, 14.
77. Elder, *Civil War Diary*, 15.
78. Elder, *Civil War Diary*, 16.
79. Ibid.
80. Ibid.
81. Ibid.

Chapter 7

82. Groom, *Vicksburg, 1863*, 58–59.
83. Groom, *Vicksburg, 1863*, 144–46.
84. Groom, *Vicksburg, 1863*, 155–57.
85. Groom, *Vicksburg, 1863*, 161.

86. Groom, *Vicksburg, 1863*, 247–48.
87. Elder, *Civil War Diary*, 18.
88. Groom, *Vicksburg, 1863*, 248–50.

Chapter 8

89. Elder, *Civil War Diary*, 19.
90. Elder, *Civil War Diary*, 20.
91. Elder, *Civil War Diary*, 24.
92. Elder, *Civil War Diary*, 25.
93. Elder, *Civil War Diary*, 26.
94. Ibid.
95. Elder, *Civil War Diary*, 27.
96. Elder, *Civil War Diary*, 28.
97. Elder, *Civil War Diary*, 31.
98. Elder, *Civil War Diary*, 32.
99. Evidently, John Taylor Moore evaded capture, for he lived in Port Gibson until his death in 1879.
100. Elder, *Civil War Diary*, 33.
101. Elder, *Civil War Diary*, 34.

Chapter 9

102. Loughborough, *My Cave Life in Vicksburg*, 19.
103. Balfour, *Mrs. Balfour's Civil War Diary*, 21.
104. Loughborough, *My Cave Life in Vicksburg*, 56–57.
105. Mother Bernard McGuire, quoted in Ellington, *Christ: The Living Water*, 450.
106. Loughborough, *My Cave Life in Vicksburg*, 63.
107. Loughborough, *My Cave Life in Vicksburg*, 141–42.
108. Loughborough, *My Cave Life in Vicksburg*, 73–74.
109. Loughborough, *My Cave Life in Vicksburg*, 77.
110. Balfour, *Mrs. Balfour's Civil War Diary*, 23.
111. "Letters Home: William Lovelace Foster."
112. Ellington, *Christ: The Living Water*, 449.
113. Loughborough, *My Cave Life in Vicksburg*, 79–80.
114. Loughborough, *My Cave Life in Vicksburg*, 91–92.
115. Loughborough, *My Cave Life in Vicksburg*, 78.
116. Balfour, *Mrs. Balfour's Civil War Diary*, 26.

117. Balfour, *Mrs. Balfour's Civil War Diary*, 25.
118. Loughborough, *My Cave Life in Vicksburg*, 137.
119. Balfour, *Mrs. Balfour's Civil War Diary*, 26.
120. Balfour, *Mrs. Balfour's Civil War Diary*, 41, and Elder, *Civil War Diary*, 55–56.

Chapter 10

121. Pillar, *Catholic Church in Mississippi*, 211–12.
122. Pillar, *Catholic Church in Mississippi*, 212–13.
123. Elder, *Civil War Diary*, 41–42.
124. Ellington, *Christ: The Living Water*, 33.
125. Elder, *Civil War Diary*, 42–43.
126. Ibid.
127. Elder, *Civil War Diary*, 43.
128. Elder, *Civil War Diary*, 44.
129. "Irish Immigrants during the U.S. Civil War."
130. Elder, *Civil War Diary*, 45.
131. Ibid.
132. Elder, *Civil War Diary*, 46.
133. Ibid.
134. Elder, *Civil War Diary*, 47.
135. Ibid.

Chapter 11

136. Sumner, *Angels of Mercy*, 21–22.
137. Elder, *Civil War Diary*, 35.
138. Sumner, *Angels of Mercy*, 22.
139. Sumner, *Angels of Mercy*, 21, footnote no. 52.
140. Sumner, *Angels of Mercy*, 22, footnote no. 53.
141. Pillar, *Catholic Church in Mississippi*, 257.
142. Gerow, *Catholicity in Mississippi*, 257.
143. Pillar, *Catholic Church in Mississippi*, 257.

Chapter 12

144. Elder, *Civil War Diary*, 47.
145. Elder, *Civil War Diary*, 48.

146. Ibid.
147. Ibid; Brinsfield, *Faith in the Fight*, 140.
148. Elder, *Civil War Diary*, 48–49.
149. Elder, *Civil War Diary*, 49.
150. Ellington, *Christ: The Living Water*, 42.
151. Ibid.
152. Elder, *Civil War Diary*, 49–50.
153. Elder, *Civil War Diary*, 50.
154. Ibid.
155. Elder, *Civil War Diary*, 51. Father Guillou died on February 7, 1863, in Natchez. Now, Elder had the task of going through Guillou's possessions that he had left behind at his residence in Vicksburg.

Chapter 13

156. Evans, *Sixteenth Mississippi Infantry*, 116–117.
157. Pillar, *Catholic Church in Mississippi*, 10–11.
158. Evans, *Sixteenth Mississippi Infantry*, 66–67.
159. Evans, *Sixteenth Mississippi Infantry*, 67.
160. Dobbins, *Grandfather's Journal*, 75.
161. Evans, *Sixteenth Mississippi Infantry*, 70.
162. Ibid.
163. Dobbins, *Grandfather's Journal*, 78.
164. Evans, *Sixteenth Mississippi Infantry*, 72.
165. Evans, *Sixteenth Mississippi Infantry*, 73.
166. Ibid.
167. Evans, *Sixteenth Mississippi Infantry*, 74.
168. Dobbins, *Grandfather's Journal*, 81.
169. Ibid.
170. Pillar, *Catholic Church in Mississippi*, 221.
171. Evans, *Sixteenth Mississippi Infantry*, 77.
172. Dobbins, *Grandfather's Journal*, 82.
173. Evans, *Sixteenth Mississippi Infantry*, 78–79.
174. Evans, *Sixteenth Mississippi Infantry*, 84.
175. Luke Ward Conerly, *A Historical Sketch of the Quitman Guards*, quoted in Evans, *Sixteenth Mississippi Infantry*, 85.
176. Evans, *Sixteenth Mississippi Infantry*, 85–87.
177. Pillar, *Catholic Church in Mississippi*, 221.
178. Evans, *Sixteenth Mississippi Infantry*, 196.

179. Evans, *Sixteenth Mississippi Infantry*, 204.

180. John Berryman Crawford, Civil War Letters Home, sites.rootsweb. com/~msjasper/military/facrawford.html, accessed 1/7/19.

181. Evans, *Sixteenth Mississippi Infantry*, 308.

Chapter 14

182. Elder, *Civil War Diary*, 51.

183. Elder, *Civil War Diary*, 52.

184. Ibid.

185. Elder, *Civil War Diary*, 53.

186. Ibid.

187. Ibid.

188. Elder, *Civil War Diary*, 54.

189. Ibid.

190. Ibid.

191. Ibid.

192. Ibid.

193. Elder, *Civil War Diary*, 55.

194. Ibid.

195. Ibid.

196. Ibid.

197. Elder, *Civil War Diary*, 56.

198. Ibid.

199. Cotton, *Horrible Outrage!*, 15.

200. Cotton, *Horrible Outrage!*, 16.

201. Cotton, *Horrible Outrage!*, 10, 16.

202. Cotton, *Horrible Outrage!*, 17.

203. Ibid.

204. Cotton, *Horrible Outrage!*, 10, 13–15.

205. Cotton, *Horrible Outrage!*, 14.

206. Cotton, *Horrible Outrage!*, 13.

207. Cotton, *Horrible Outrage!*, 19.

208. Ibid.

209. Cotton, *Horrible Outrage!*, 8.

210. Cotton, *Horrible Outrage!*, 7.

211. Cotton, *Horrible Outrage!*, 21.

212. Cotton, *Horrible Outrage!*, 22–23.

213. Cotton, *Horrible Outrage!*, 24–25.

214. Cotton, *Horrible Outrage!*, 25.

215. *Vicksburg Herald*, plaque found in Old Depot Museum, Vicksburg, Mississippi.

216. Cotton, *Horrible Outrage!*, 37.

217. Cotton, *Horrible Outrage!*, 12.

218. Cotton, *Horrible Outrage!*, 10.

219. Cotton, *Horrible Outrage!*, 37.

220. Cotton, *Horrible Outrage!*, 38.

221. Ibid.

222. Ibid.

223. Elder, *Civil War Diary*, 56.

224. Ibid.

225. Ibid.

226. Elder, *Civil War Diary*, 56–57.

227. Elder, *Civil War Diary*, 57.

228. Ibid.

229. Ibid.

230. Ibid.

231. Cotton and Giambrone, *Vicksburg and the War*, 57.

232. Elder, *Civil War Diary*, 58.

233. Ibid.

234. "The World Turned Upside Down" was the tune British general Charles Cornwallis allegedly had played when his troops evacuated Yorktown, Virginia, after surrendering to George Washington's army. Many Confederates saw themselves as the inheritors of Washington's Revolution. Now, it was their own "world turned upside down."

235. Henry David Thoreau quoted in "Interview on C.S. Lewis."

236. Elder, *Civil War Diary*, 58.

237. Ibid.

238. Elder, *Civil War Diary*, 59.

239. Ibid.

240. Elder, *Civil War Diary*, 60.

241. Ibid.

242. "Contraband" was the designation given by the Federal government to slaves who left their masters and fled to Union lines. The Federal government refused to acknowledge the Confederacy as a legitimate government. Therefore, the runaway slaves were legally still property. Only, now, they were "captured property," or contraband.

243. Elder, *Civil War Diary*, 60.

244. Ibid.
245. Elder, *Civil War Diary*, 61.
246. Ibid.
247. Elder, *Civil War Diary*, 62.
248. A scapular is a Catholic article of devotion worn about the shoulders. Its intent is to remind the wearer of his duty to live his life in imitation of Christ.
249. Elder, *Civil War Diary*, 63.
250. Ibid.
251. Ibid.
252. Ibid.
253. Ibid.
254. Elder, *Civil War Diary*, 64.
255. Ibid.
256. Ibid.
257. Ibid.

Chapter 15

258. Cumming, *Journal of a Confederate Nurse*, 10.
259. Cumming, *Journal of a Confederate Nurse*, 12.
260. Cumming, *Journal of a Confederate Nurse*, 14.
261. Cumming, *Journal of a Confederate Nurse*, 15.
262. Cumming, *Journal of a Confederate Nurse*, 16.
263. Cumming, *Journal of a Confederate Nurse*, 19.
264. Cumming, *Journal of a Confederate Nurse*, 20.
265. Cumming, *Journal of a Confederate Nurse*, 20–21.
266. Cumming, *Journal of a Confederate Nurse*, 21.
267. Ibid.
268. Cumming, *Journal of a Confederate Nurse*, 25.
269. Ibid.
270. Ibid.
271. Cumming, *Journal of a Confederate Nurse*, 26.
272. Ibid.
273. Cumming, *Journal of a Confederate Nurse*, 32.
274. Ibid.
275. Cumming, *Journal of a Confederate Nurse*, 44.
276. Cumming, *Journal of a Confederate Nurse*, 45.

Chapter 16

277. Elder, *Civil War Diary*, 65–66.

278. Elder, *Civil War Diary*, 66.

279. Elder, *Civil War Diary*, 67.

280. Ibid.

281. Elder, *Civil War Diary*, 68.

282. Elder, *Civil War Diary*, 69. Unfortunately, Elder does not tell us if this visit from the Union general was related to the incident at the orphanage.

283. Elder, *Civil War Diary*, 69–70.

284. General Sherman wrote this in a letter to Ellen Ewing Sherman on January 28, 1863: "Here we are at Vicksburg on the wrong side of the river trying to turn the Mississippi by a ditch, a pure waste of human labor."

285. Cotton and Giambrone, *Vicksburg and the War*, 34.

286. Cotton and Giambrone, *Vicksburg and the War*, 33.

287. Pillar, *Catholic Church in Mississippi*, 224–225.

288. Cotton and Giambrone, *Vicksburg and the War*, 121.

289. Ibid.

290. Cotton and Mason, *With Malice Toward Some*, 7.

291. Harper, *Annie Harper's Journal*.

292. One, justifiably, should say "indefensible racist views aside." Yet, Annie Harper's (errant) view of black people does bring into question the role of the black man in the post-Emancipation United States. If so many black people were enslaved by the Southern half of their nation and abandoned by the Northern half, what would their future be after the—supposedly their—country was reunified?

293. Elder, *Civil War Diary*, 70.

294. Matt. 25:40.

295. Richard Gerow, quoted in Elder, *Civil War Diary*, 71.

Chapter 17

296. Elder, *Civil War Diary*, 72.

297. Ibid.

298. Ibid.

299. Elder, *Civil War Diary*, 73.

300. Ibid.

301. Ibid.

302. Elder, *Civil War Diary*, 74.
303. Pillar, *Catholic Church in Mississippi*, 234.
304. Elder, *Civil War Diary*, 75.
305. Ibid.
306. Elder, *Civil War Diary*, 76.
307. Ibid.
308. Ibid.
309. Elder, *Civil War Diary*, 77.
310. Ibid.
311. Elder, *Civil War Diary*, 78.
312. Ibid.
313. Ibid.
314. Ibid.
315. Elder, *Civil War Diary*, 79.
316. Ibid.
317. Elder, *Civil War Diary*, 81.
318. Woodrick, *Civil War Siege of Jackson*, 55.
319. Elder, *Civil War Diary*, 79.
320. Elder, *Civil War Diary*, 79–80.
321. Ellington, *Christ: The Living Water*, 43.
322. The Civil War in the East, 18th Mississippi Infantry Regiment.
323. Elder, *Civil War Diary*, 80.
324. Ibid.
325. Elder, *Civil War Diary*, 80–81.
326. Elder, *Civil War Diary*, 81.
327. Elder, *Civil War Diary*, 82.
328. Ibid.
329. Elder, *Civil War Diary*, 82–83.
330. Elder, *Civil War Diary*, 83.
331. Ibid.
332. Elder, *Civil War Diary*, 43.
333. Elder, *Civil War Diary*, 83–84.
334. Elder, *Civil War Diary*, 84.
335. Ibid.
336. Elder, *Civil War Diary*, 85.
337. Ibid.
338. Ibid.
339. Elder, *Civil War Diary*, 86.
340. Ibid.

341. Ibid.
342. Elder, *Civil War Diary*, 87.
343. Ibid.
344. Ibid.
345. Ibid.
346. Ibid.
347. Elder, *Civil War Diary*, 87–88.
348. Elder, *Civil War Diary*, 88.
349. Ibid.
350. Ibid.

Chapter 18

351. Elder, *Civil War Diary*, 89–90.
352. Elder, *Civil War Diary*, 90.
353. Ibid.
354. Elder, *Civil War Diary*, 90–91.
355. Elder, *Civil War Diary*, 91.
356. Ibid.
357. Ibid.
358. Elder, *Civil War Diary*, 92.
359. Ibid.
360. Ibid.
361. Elder, *Civil War Diary*, 93.
362. Ibid.
363. Ibid.
364. Elder, *Civil War Diary*, 93–94.
365. Elder, *Civil War Diary*, 94.
366. Ibid.
367. Ibid.
368. Ibid.
369. Elder, *Civil War Diary*, 95.
370. Ibid.
371. Elder, *Civil War Diary*, 96.
372. Ibid.
373. Elder, *Civil War Diary*, 96–97.
374. Elder, *Civil War Diary*, 97.
375. Ibid.
376. Elder, *Civil War Diary*, 97–98.

377. Elder, *Civil War Diary*, 98.
378. Ibid.
379. Elder, *Civil War Diary*, 99.
380. Ibid.
381. Elder, *Civil War Diary*, 100.
382. Ibid.
383. Elder, *Civil War Diary*, 100–101.
384. Ibid.
385. Elder, *Civil War Diary*, 101.
386. Elder, *Civil War Diary*, 102.
387. Ibid.
388. Ibid.
389. Elder, *Civil War Diary*, 103.
390. Ibid.
391. Elder, *Civil War Diary*, 125.
392. Elder, *Civil War Diary*, 104.

Chapter 19

393. Ibid.
394. Elder, *Civil War Diary*, 105.
395. Ibid.
396. Elder, *Civil War Diary*, 106.
397. Elder, *Civil War Diary*, 107.
398. Elder, *Civil War Diary*, 108.
399. Elder, *Civil War Diary*, 110.
400. Elder, *Civil War Diary*, 109.
401. Elder, *Civil War Diary*, 111.
402. Elder, *Civil War Diary*, 112.
403. Ibid.
404. Elder, *Civil War Diary*, 112–13.
405. Elder, *Civil War Diary*, 113.
406. Ibid.
407. Elder, *Civil War Diary*, 114.
408. Ibid.

Chapter 20

409. Cotton and Giambrone, *Vicksburg and the War*, 107, 109.
410. Cotton and Mason, *With Malice Toward Some*, 10.
411. Cotton and Giambrone, *Vicksburg and the War*, 109–13.
412. Elder, *Civil War Diary*, 81.
413. Cotton and Giambrone, *Vicksburg and the War*, 114.

Chapter 21

414. Elder, *Civil War Diary*, 115–16.
415. Elder, *Civil War Diary*, 116.
416. Ibid.
417. Pillar, *Catholic Church in Mississippi*, 289, note 144.
418. Elder, *Civil War Diary*, 116.
419. Elder, *Civil War Diary*, 116–17.
420. Pillar, *Catholic Church in Mississippi*, 288.
421. Elder, *Civil War Diary*, 117.
422. Ibid.
423. Elder, *Civil War Diary*, 117–18.
424. Elder, *Civil War Diary*, 118.
425. Ibid.
426. Elder, *Civil War Diary*, 119.
427. Ibid.
428. Elder, *Civil War Diary*, 120.
429. Ibid.
430. Ibid.

WORKS CITED

ARTICLES

Broussard, Joyce L. "Occupied Natchez, Elite Women, and the Feminization of the Civil War." *Journal of Mississippi History* 70 (2008).

BOOKS

An English Combatant. *Battle-Fields of the South*. Alexandria, VA: Time Life Books, 1984.

Balfour, Emma Harrison. *Mrs. Balfour's Civil War Diary: A Personal Account of the Siege of Vicksburg By Emma Balfour*. Vicksburg, MS: Gordon A. Cotton, 2008.

Beagle, Donald Robert, and Bryan Albin Giemza. *Poet of the Lost Cause: A Life of Father Ryan*. Knoxville: University of Tennessee Press, 2008.

Bernard, Mary. *The Story of the Sisters of Mercy in Mississippi 1860–1930*. New York: P.J. Kennedy & Sons, 1931.

Brinsfield, John W., William C. Davis, Benedict Maryniak and James I. Robertson Jr., eds. *Faith in the Fight: Civil War Chaplains*. Mechanicsburg, PA: Stackpole Books, 2003.

Chernow, Ron. *Grant*. New York: Penguin Press, 2017.

Cooper, William J., Jr. *Jefferson Davis, American*. New York: Alfred A. Knopf, 2000.

Cotton, Gordon A. *Horrible Outrage! The Murder of Minerva Cook*. Vicksburg, MS: Self-published, 1993.

Cotton, Gordon A., and Jeff Giambrone. *Vicksburg and the War*. Gretna, LA: Pelican Publishing Company, 2004.

Cotton, Gordon A., and Ralph C. Mason. *With Malice Toward Some: The Military Occupation of Vicksburg, 1864–1865*. Vicksburg, MS: Vicksburg and Warren County Historical Society, 1991.

Cumming, Kate. *Kate: The Journal of a Confederate Nurse*. Edited by Richard Barksdale Harwell. Baton Rouge: Louisiana State University Press, 1959.

Dobbins, Austin C. *Grandfather's Journal: Company B, Sixteenth Mississippi Infantry Volunteers, Harris' Brigade, Mahone's Division, Hill's Corps, A.N.V. May 27, 1861–July 15, 1865*. Dayton, OH: Morningside House, 1988.

Elder, William Henry. *Character-Glimpses of Most Reverend William Henry Elder, D.D.: Second Archbishop of Cincinnati*. New York: Frederick Pustet & Company, 1911.

———. *Civil War Diary (1862–1865) of Bishop William Henry Elder, Bishop of Natchez*. Natchez, MS: Most Reverend R.O. Gerow, 1960?.

Ellington, Cleta. *Christ: The Living Water: The Catholic Church in Mississippi*. Jackson: Mississippi Today, 1989.

Evans, Robert G., ed. *The Sixteenth Mississippi Infantry: Civil War Letters and Reminiscences*. Jackson: University Press of Mississippi, 2002.

Gerow, Richard Oliver, ed. *Catholicity in Mississippi*. Marrero, LA: Hope Haven Press, 1939.

Groom, Winston. *Shiloh, 1862*. Washington, D.C.: National Geographic Society, 2012.

———. *Vicksburg, 1863*. New York: Alfred A. Knopf, 2009.

Harper, Annie. *Annie Harper's Journal: A Southern Mother's Legacy*. Denton, TX: Flower Mound Writing Company, 1983.

Loughborough, Mary Ann Webster. *My Cave Life in Vicksburg*. Charlotte, NC: Strait Gate Publications, 2014.

Pillar, James J. *The Catholic Church in Mississippi, 1837–1865*. New Orleans: The Hauser Press, 1964.

Sumner, Ignatius. *Angels of Mercy: An Eyewitness Account, A Primary Source by Sister Ignatius Sumner of the Civil War and Yellow Fever*. Edited by Sister Paulinus Oakes. Baltimore, MD: Catholic Foundation Press, 1998.

Woodrick, Jim. *The Civil War Siege of Jackson, Mississippi*. Charleston, SC: The History Press, 2016.

Wynne, Ben. *Mississippi's Civil War: A Narrative History*. Macon, GA: Mercer University Press, 2006.

Dissertations and Theses

Vaughan, William Ashley. "Natchez During the Civil War." PhD diss., University of Southern Mississippi, 2001.
White, Ruth Poe. "A Tale of Two Cities: Vicksburg and Natchez, Mississippi During the American Civil War." Master's thesis, University of Southern Mississippi, 2014.

Manuscripts

Elder Letter Book. Mississippi Department of Archives and History.
William Henry Elder. Subject File Mississippi Department of Archives and History.

Newspapers

Mississippi Free Trader (Natchez).
Natchez Daily Courier.
Sea Coast Echo.
Vicksburg Herald.

Websites

The Civil War in the East, 18th Mississippi Infantry Regiment. civilwarintheeast.com.
"Interview on C.S. Lewis." www.peterkreeft.com.
"Irish Immigrants during the U.S. Civil War." immigrationtounitedstates.org.
"Letters Home: William Lovelace Foster." www.nps.gov.
Newspapers.com.

About the Author

Ryan Starrett was birthed and reared in Jackson, Mississippi. After receiving degrees from the University of Dallas, Spring Hill College and Adams State University, as well as spending a ten-year hiatus in Texas, he has returned home to continue his teaching career. *Mississippi Bishop William Henry Elder and the Civil War* is Ryan's first solo project. He also coauthored, with Josh Foreman, *Hidden History of Jackson*, *Hidden History of the Mississippi Sound* and *Hidden History of New Orleans* (coming in January 2020). Their website can be found at foremanstarrett.com.